PENNY JUNOR

QUEEN ELIZABETH II

1952 · 1992

A PICTORIAL CELEBRATION OF HER REIGN

BCA

LONDON · NEW YORK · SYDNEY · TORONTO

DEDICATION

~

For my mother-in-law, Peggy, who saw her crowned and has not missed a Christmas broadcast in 40 years.

~

*This edition published 1991
by BCA by arrangement with
CONRAN OCTOPUS LIMITED*

*First published in 1991 by
Conran Octopus Limited
37 Shelton Street
London WC2H 9HN*

CN 2985

*Designer: Peter Bridgewater
Project Editor: Simon Willis
Copy Editor: Jane Royston
Picture Researcher: Celia Dearing
Production Manager: Sonya Sibbons*

Typeset by Central Southern Typesetters, Eastbourne

*Printed and bound in Great Britain by Butler & Tanner Ltd,
Frome and London*

PAGE 1: the Queen and the Duke of Edinburgh with Prince Charles and Princess Anne in the grounds of Windsor Castle, 1952.

~

PAGE 2: Queen Elizabeth, the Queen Mother, the Queen, and the Prince and Princess of Wales after the christening of Prince Harry, 1984.

~

PAGES 4-5: The royal family watching the traditional fly-past from the balcony of Buckingham Palace during the annual Trooping the Colour ceremony which marks the Queen's official birthday, June 1991. Bad weather kept the eight Tornado jets, which had taken part in the Gulf conflict, on the ground, leaving three veteran Shackletons with the sky to themselves. The motto of the 40-year-old planes is 'Old age and treachery will triumph over youth and skill'.

Introduction

QUEEN ELIZABETH II is the most influential, the most famous and probably the wealthiest woman alive. She is also the most extraordinary. She is enormously influential, yet she has no power. Her face is known to everyone, yet she herself remains an enigma. She is rich beyond most people's wildest dreams, yet she and her family are maintained at public expense. As head of state, she understands more about politics than do most politicians, yet she remains silent on the subject and shares her thoughts with no one. Her role is highly illogical, and some would say that in this day and age it is irrelevant too. Yet despite all the illogicalities, the monarchy in Britain is more secure now than it has been at any time in history.

Looking at the familiar and friendly face of the Queen as she clasps the hand of a grandchild, urges on a horse at the Derby, or laughs over a private joke, it is tempting to think that Elizabeth II is just like any other woman in her mid-sixties, with a love of the countryside and a penchant for hats and headscarves. She looks so very ordinary, so normal, so unremarkable; and had it not been for a quirk of fate when she was a girl, she might indeed have been as ordinary as she looks.

It was the sudden abdication of her uncle that so dramatically altered Elizabeth's life. She was just ten

THE YOUNG Princess Elizabeth (above, with her baby, Anne, in 1951) little knew how soon she would have to juggle the roles of wife and mother with the responsibilities of state.

when Edward VIII gave up the throne to marry the American divorcee Wallis Simpson in December 1936, less than ten months after becoming King. Elizabeth's father was left to pick up the pieces and to restore the nation's shattered confidence. The prospect of continuing life privately and peacefully as minor royals vanished, and the quiet family was rudely thrust into the public eye. George VI was shy and ill-equipped for the job, and the strain of it cost him his life, bringing Elizabeth to the throne decades earlier than anyone might have expected. But King George did achieve a turnaround in the monarchy's popularity, and his eldest daughter has capitalized and built on this.

Elsewhere in Europe, crowned heads have been falling like ninepins. As Albert I of the Belgians once said, 'There's a lot of unemployment in my profession.' Four emperors and eleven kings have lost their thrones since the First World War. Yet the monarchy in Britain has seldom enjoyed such esteem as it does today. Despite attacks in the House of Commons from left-wing MPs, most notably Willie Hamilton, the republican movement has few supporters. The vast majority of people in Britain love and support and value their Queen, as opinion polls show time and time again. They love her because she brings a touch of magic and mystery into people's lives, giving them a sense of identity, of national pride, and a feeling of continuity. Their world may be crumbling, unemployment may be high, the country may be at war or in the grip of a recession, but the sight of the Queen still going about her work, concerned but otherwise unperturbed by events, provides a curious sense of security and optimism, a knowledge that life will go on, that these difficulties will pass. She is like the parent who is always there to depend on, keeping calm in times of panic, and betraying none of her emotions to the outside world.

Unlike presidents who come and go, and are reliant upon votes to remain in office, the Queen is a fixture, and is motivated by no desire or need to please any particular faction. She remains utterly impartial, motivated only by the welfare of her subjects, and the safe keeping of all that she has pledged to guard.

And that is the very essence of her success. Frederick the Great once said that a crown was nothing more than a hat that let the rain in. Queen Elizabeth II believes very differently. She believes that when she was anointed Queen, it was a sacred moment, a moment that spiritually set her apart from the rest of humanity; and that the crown is a symbol of that high office to which she was appointed by God. That is what has kept her going throughout the long and often troubled years of her reign: her sincere belief that she has a duty to discharge with her life.

King Farouk of Egypt, who was forced to abdicate by the army in the same year Elizabeth II came to the throne in Britain, commented on his predicament that 'There will soon be only five kings left – the kings of England, Diamonds, Hearts, Spades and Clubs.' However, it is not just that the British are sentimental about their historical traditions. Britain's constitutional monarchy – embodied in the Queen, and the envy of the world – is safe because she has rightly judged the tone and the conduct and the style that is appropriate for the job. Elizabeth has not been tempted to bow to pressure from any quarter, nor to change her image to suit any whim of fashion. She chooses sensible, comfortable clothes that neither distract nor detract, that change imperceptibly with the years, and that complement every occasion. She has not been persuaded in our 'see-through' society to sparkle especially for the camera, to inject false charisma into her speeches, or to let the public into her private life. She won't perform, because she does not perceive that as her role. To show emotion on formal occasions would be to detract from the solemnity of her office.

The media have tried hard to turn her family into characters from a soap opera, and some of the younger

THE QUEEN watches a polo match at Smith's Lawn, Windsor (left). For the entire length of her career, Elizabeth has found herself presenting polo cups to members of her family, first to Prince Philip and later to Prince Charles.

members have taken the cue more willingly than others, but the Queen remains almost untouched by gossip. She remains enigmatic, special and mystical. And while rumour has run rife and scandal erupted from time to time about various members of her family, she herself has been left unscathed, behaved impeccably, and, apart from the occasional sharp word to a photographer, she has done nothing in forty years to shake the belief that so many of her subjects have in her, that she is in some way superhuman.

Yet the humour and the personality are there, as the camera so often reveals, and the occasional story. There was the time some years ago, for example, when the Queen and Princess Anne were being driven down the Mall from Buckingham Palace when a young and very green police officer flagged down their driver and asked to see his licence. The policeman had evidently failed to notice the insignia and was obviously quite unaware that this was a royal car. The driver, hoping to spare the policeman embarrassment, motioned over his shoulder, in an effort to warn him that he had just flagged down his sovereign Queen. The rookie failed to take the hint and stolidly proceeded with his business. The Queen and her daughter meanwhile slid down on to the floor in the back of the car, to keep out of view. Their driver continued to gesticulate wildly that the officer should check out the back before writing out his ticket. At last the light dawned and the policeman walked to the back of the car and, pressing his face against the window, looked inside. On finding himself eye to eye with the familiar face of his monarch crouching behind the seats, his wish that the ground should open up and swallow

him was clearly granted, because he vanished into thin air and was neither seen nor heard of again.

The Queen takes a lot of pleasure in her family. She is pleased with and proud of them all, and there is no doubt that not being there to watch them grow up was one of the greatest sacrifices she had to make in becoming Queen. She was just twenty-five when the King, her father, died. Her children were four and two years old, her husband an officer in the Navy, and she could have expected ten or twenty years ahead of her in which to be a naval wife and bring up her children. Instead the family's life was turned upside down.

Elizabeth was in Kenya when she heard the news of the King's death. When she arrived home, her first visitor was Queen Mary, who curtsied as they met. 'Her old Grannie and subject must be the first to kiss her hand,' she said. From that day on, protocol insists that everyone must curtsy or bow in her presence, even her mother, her husband and her children. In public everyone must call her 'Ma'am', walk two paces behind her, speak only when spoken to, and retreat backwards from her presence.

The following day, 7 February, she met her Privy Council, and, looking very pale, read out the declaration of accession, saying, 'My heart is too full for me to say more to you today than that I shall always work as my father did.' The next morning at 11 o'clock the Garter King of Arms stood on the balcony of St James's Palace and proclaimed that

. . . the High and Mighty Princess Elizabeth Alexandra Mary is now, by the Death of our late

Sovereign of Happy Memory, become Queen Elizabeth the Second, by the Grace of God Queen of this Realm and of all her other Realms and Territories, Head of the Commonwealth, Defender of the Faith, to whom Her lieges do acknowledge all Faith and constant Obedience, with hearty and humble Affection; beseeching God, by whom Kings and Queens do reign, to bless the Royal Queen Elizabeth the Second with long and happy years to reign over us.

In that single proclamation a young mother lost her freedom, and at a stroke became head of the greatest group of nations in history, as well as one of the loneliest women on earth. Elizabeth became Supreme Governor of the Church of England, Supreme Commander of the Armed Forces and Head of the Executive, the Legislature, and the Judiciary. All government is, therefore, carried out in her name: its ministers are her ministers. They can advise her on courses of action, but they are dependent upon her consent before any bill can become an Act of Parliament. In practice, however, their advice is not open to debate, and her approval is a formality; she has no right of veto. Under the unwritten constitution of Great Britain, today's sovereign cannot govern or command: she does not rule, she reigns; and her role is fundamentally symbolic. She does still retain the right to dissolve Parliament, although in practice she does that on the advice of her prime minister. She also retains the right to choose her prime minister, but her choice is invariably the leader of the largest party in the House of Commons.

Yet though the role may be symbolic, Britain's constitutional monarchy is one of her most valuable assets, in part because it has so little political power, and thus remains a constant in an ever-changing world.

As life has changed, the Queen has remained constant. In some ways she has filled the gap left by religion; provided an icon, if not for worship, at least for people to look up to as a reflection of all that is best in human nature. To millions of her subjects she stands for the values that Christianity represents.

Elizabeth has increasingly become a Queen of the people, seeming to delight in contact with the general public. They feel, furthermore, that she is theirs. She may be rich and privileged beyond people's wildest dreams, she may live in a remote world of castles and palaces, but she has so presented herself to people that they feel they can appeal to her for help, often when the authorities – her government or her courts – have turned them away. In the early 1970s she began the custom of the royal walkabout, which is now built into almost every royal programme, so much so that it is hard to remember a time when members of the royal family didn't stop to talk to the crowd. Previously the Queen met only those people who were formally presented to her; now, the public can see something of the woman, the human face of monarchy. It has done a great deal to cement public affection, and allows her subjects to feel, as Harold Nicolson said about Queen Victoria, 'that in any crisis she was weeping the same salt tears into the same over-strong tea as they were.'

The practice of walkabouts is a nightmare for those responsible for her security. The Queen is obviously a

STATE VISITS made by the Queen to countries as diverse as the USSR, Hong Kong and Saudi Arabia help to cement diplomatic ties and to secure trade deals. Seen here visiting Washington, D.C. in 1991 (right), the Queen's hectic schedule shows little sign of slowing down as she reaches an age at which almost all women have passed retirement.

plum target for any number of terrorist organizations, and she is clearly vulnerable walking amongst crowds of people on the street. President Kennedy of the USA, and President Sadat of Egypt, Prime Minister Indira Gandhi and her son, Rajiv, were all shot dead or blown up; Pope John Paul II and President Reagan were shot and wounded; and closer to home, Lord Mountbatten and MPs Airey Neave and Ian Gow were killed by terrorist bombs. Even the Queen has had close shaves. A man in the crowd fired a gun during the Trooping the Colour ceremony in 1981. It was filled with blank cartridges, but they could have been real bullets. And there have been several intruders who have found their way into the grounds of Buckingham Palace, including one, Michael Fagan, who in July 1982 gained entry to the Queen's bedroom.

Unnerving as such incidents have been, it is very much the Queen's decision to continue with the style of monarchy that she has established. She listens to the advice she is offered, and takes sensible precautions, but is adamant, like her government, that to alter her way of life because of the threat of terrorism would be to concede victory to those who live by violence.

Her life revolves around a routine that scarcely differs from one year to the next. There are several distinct areas of responsibility inherent in her string of titles. As head of state, she has to endorse the routine of government, read state papers which arrive daily, and give her assent to proposed bills. She also meets her Prime Minister regularly to discuss the week's business. She travels abroad as Britain's ambassador, and receives visiting heads of state at home. There are

traditional ceremonies throughout the year that appear as fixtures in her diary, which combine her role as Defender of the Faith and public figurehead: she leads the worship on Remembrance Day, for example. She holds investitures to bestow honours on those citizens who have distinguished themselves; and she keeps herself in touch with her less-distinguished citizens by visiting schools, hospitals and factories around the country, and meeting ordinary people. She holds a series of garden parties at Buckingham Palace every summer, and there are sporting and entertainment fixtures too: Royal Ascot, for example, the Derby, the Royal Tournament and the Royal Variety Performance. There is the ceremonial, too, such as the State Opening of Parliament, the Trooping the Colour on her official birthday in June each year, and the distribution of Maundy money on the day before Good Friday. As head of the Armed Forces, the Queen also has a duty to inspect her troops stationed around the world. Additionally, there is her role as Head of the Commonwealth, which involves entirely separate duties.

Official engagements are mapped out at least six months in advance, foreign tours even longer, and plans are very seldom altered. Holidays play a central part, too, and likewise follow a traditional pattern. The Queen decamps to Scotland in August and stays there for several weeks, surrounded by most members of her family. She spends Christmas at Windsor Castle or Sandringham, and is at Sandringham in any event for the New Year, and for the pheasant shooting.

It is on holiday, buried in the countryside, surrounded by dogs and horses, that the Queen is happiest; and it is here that she relaxes, here where the private woman appears, the one who loves to put on wellington boots and a headscarf, and spend her day walking, stalking, fishing, or riding. By night, she insists upon dressing formally for dinner, but loves playing party games, and does wicked impersonations of politicians and statesmen that can reduce her family, and close friends who visit, to uncontrollable mirth.

Her major passion, however, is horse-racing, and she is one of the most knowledgeable race-goers and breeders of racehorses in the country. The Queen now has approaching twenty horses in training, a further twenty or so brood mares, and fifteen yearlings, as well as a substantial shareholding in two first-class stallions. It is big business, financed entirely by the Queen's private money. Her racing manager, Lord Porchester, owner of the famous Highclere Stud, is an old friend, and has been overseeing her interests for more than twenty years. He is frequently at her side during races, and telephones regularly to keep her informed. Most of the Queen's horses are based at the Sandringham and Wolferton Studs in East Anglia; she also has horses in training at two stables in Berkshire. But the Queen is no armchair owner. She knows her horses very well, often gets up at the crack of dawn to drive to the downs and watch them exercise, helps choose the best sire for her mares, and, if she is in the right place at the right time, is there when they foal. She is also there when they run, if her timetable possibly permits, and she watches a lot of racing on television.

The love of horses unites most of her family, and if the Queen is not watching racing in her leisure time, she is watching some other sort of equestrian event. Prince Philip was a keen polo player for many years. He was introduced to the sport in 1950 by his uncle, Lord Mountbatten, and played fanatically until arthritis in his left hand forced him to give it up in favour of driving four-in-hand. Prince Charles took over where his father left off, so the Queen has found herself presenting prizes to one or other member of her family for the entire length of her reign. Princess Anne has taken her share of prizes from her mother too. Her obsession was three-day eventing, another difficult and dangerous activity, at which she excelled.

Curiously, the Queen's two younger children, Prince Andrew and Prince Edward, have no such enthusiasm. Both can ride – they would be outcasts in the family if they couldn't – but neither has taken it up seriously. Prince Andrew's principal passion is photography, which he has no doubt picked up from his mother, and other members of the family: the Queen has been a keen photographer all her adult life, and a camera slung around her neck is almost as familiar a sight as the headscarf. Edward has taken up another family enthusiasm: the theatre. In the early 1940s, the Queen and her sister appeared in a succession of nativity plays and pantomimes; and she still loves to play charades. Prince Charles is also a frustrated thespian. He appeared on the stage at school, and joined the famous Cambridge Footlights at university.

Yet despite this enthusiasm, the Queen is not a great theatre-goer, nor is she particularly fond of either opera or ballet. Her choice of entertainment is apparently very ordinary. There is nothing low-brow about her taste in art, however. She has the most distinguished collection of paintings in private ownership, which was begun by George IV. It contains priceless works by artists including Michelangelo, Leonardo da Vinci, Canaletto, Van Dyck and Holbein. She also has an extremely valuable stamp collection built up by Georges V and VI, a collection of priceless antique French furniture and, of course, the famous crown jewels, which run to more than a quarter of a million separate items.

These collections actually belong to the nation, but the Queen personally owns plenty more, and is still without doubt the richest woman in the world. She owns vast amounts of land and property including large tracts of London, plus fifty-two thousand acres in the Duchy of Lancaster, most of which is actually in Yorkshire. She also owns the estates at Sandringham and Balmoral, and the racecourse at Ascot. But the bulk of her money comes from her carefully managed investments. The size of her personal fortune is undisclosed, but recent estimates have put her daily income from her investments as high as £1.8 million. Nobody will ever know the real figure.

Yet despite her fabulous wealth the Queen has never been ostentatious. She lives a comparatively frugal life in private. The state rooms at Buckingham Palace may be all you would expect in the foremost building in the land: the vast rooms where banquets and investitures are held, and visiting kings and potentates entertained, are grandly ornate; but the family apartments and the offices that house the hundreds of people who work there are surprisingly plain, and in parts quite shabby. Carpets are threadbare and walls in need of new paint.

There is an air of austerity in all her homes.

This is a hangover, perhaps, from her own childhood experience of wartime Britain. When Elizabeth came to the throne the country was still suffering austerity after the ravages of World War II. Nearly five million people had no plumbed-in bath, nearly a million had no inside toilet, and more than half a million had no running water. Food rationing remained in operation. It was a very different country from the Britain of today, where most families have two cars, fitted kitchens and holiday abroad each summer. Britain still had an Empire. Malta and Cyprus were British colonies; and there were no independent states in black Africa, in the Caribbean or in South-East Asia that had formerly belonged to Britain. Elizabeth became sovereign of six countries – the United Kingdom, Canada, Australia, New Zealand, Ceylon and South Africa. The Commonwealth consisted of those six countries plus the republics of India and Pakistan.

The Queen has seen the Empire dismantled and Britain's influence diminish, yet curiously her own status as a unifying figure at the head of the Commonwealth has grown dramatically. Today it has a membership of forty-nine countries. Twenty-three are monarchies, of which eighteen owe allegiance to the Queen; and although the Queen has no prerogatives in her role as head of the Commonwealth, she nevertheless has enormous influence.

She holds the post, not as British head of state, but as impartial figurehead, and, as a result, she has been able to build up a relationship of trust and friendship with its leaders, and act as a unifying force amongst a band of widely differing temperaments, cultures and religions.

Forty years after her accession, Elizabeth II can look back with pride at a job well done. Now past the age when most women retire, she has a successor trained, ready and waiting, and yet the likelihood that she will step down and hand over the crown to the Prince of Wales is remote. The Queen has pledged her life to the service of her people.

She was just twenty-one when she broadcast a 'very simple' message to the Commonwealth, in which she said, 'I declare before you all that my whole life, whether it be long or short, shall be devoted to your service and the service of our great Imperial Commonwealth to which we all belong.' While she has the strength still in her, and her wits about her, that is no less than she will give.

A LONE WOMAN surrounded by the pageantry and splendour of state (above), the Queen sits in her landau during the Trooping the Colour ceremony.

1952

N̶o one knows the precise time at which Princess Elizabeth became sovereign. George VI died in his sleep in the early morning of 6 February, and it was only when his valet failed to wake the sleeping King, that anyone knew he was dead. He was just fifty-six. The news, when Philip broke it to Elizabeth 4,000 miles away in Kenya, was a cruel shock. She had lost a father of whom she was deeply fond; but she had also been trained and prepared for this moment for much of her life, and, as her staff prepared to leave, she refused to show the grief she obviously felt.

The new Queen and her husband returned to a country in mourning. That night the Prime Minister, Winston Churchill, broadcast a tribute to the dead King. He ended with stirring oratory, reminiscent of his finest wartime speeches: 'I, whose youth was passed in the august, unchallenged and tranquil glories of the Victorian era, may well feel a thrill in invoking once more the prayer and the anthem, "God Save the Queen".'

ELIZABETH returning home in mourning (below). Waiting, in order of precedence, to greet their new sovereign are, from right to left: her Prime Minister, Winston Churchill; Leader of the Opposition, Clement Atlee; Secretary of State for Foreign Affairs, Anthony Eden; and the Lord President of the Council, Lord Woolton. The Queen arrived in mourning: she and every member of the royal family always travel with a suitable outfit in case there is a sudden death and they have to return quickly.

DURING ONE OF her last days as a carefree Princess (right) Elizabeth leans forward to talk to a little African boy called Prince, named after Prince Charles, with whom he shared a birthday. She and the Duke of Edinburgh were in Nairobi, Kenya, on the first leg of a tour of the Commonwealth. They had intended to be away for five months, but in the event they were on African soil for less than a week when word came, on 6 February, that the King was dead. They had spent that night at Treetops, a hunting lodge on the Aberdare game reserve, watching animals drink from a watering-hole.

THREE QUEENS in
mourning (left): Queen
Elizabeth II, Queen Mary,
and Queen Elizabeth, now
Queen Mother, wait outside
Westminster Hall to pay
their last respects to the
body of King George VI.
Between them they had lost a
beloved father, a son and a
husband, and there was no
disguising their grief. The
next day the King was buried
in St George's Chapel,
Windsor, and as his coffin
was lowered into the ground,
the entire country observed
two minutes' silence.
Tributes flowed in from all
over the world. In a message
of thanks, the Queen Mother
said, 'Your concern for me
has upheld me in my sorrow
. . . No man had a deeper
sense than he of duty and of
service, and no man was full
of more compassion for his
fellow men. He loved you
all, every one of you most
truly.' Then she said, 'I
commend to you our dear
daughter: give her your
loyalty and devotion, in the
great and lonely station to
which she has been called.
She will need your protection
and love. God bless you all,
and may He in His wisdom
guide us safely to our true
destiny of peace and
goodwill.'

N E W S
IN BRIEF
~

7 Jan – General Dwight Eisenhower, Supreme Allied Commander in Europe, declares that he is prepared to run for President of the USA

31 Jan – Princess Elizabeth and the Duke of Edinburgh leave for a tour of Commonwealth countries

6 Feb – King George VI dies peacefully in his sleep

8 Feb – Elizabeth returns from Kenya and is proclaimed Queen

21 Feb – Identity cards are abolished in Britain

26 Feb – Churchill tells the House of Commons that Britain has nuclear capabilities

9 Apr – The Queen says that the Royal Family will retain the name Windsor

22 Apr – The US explodes its most powerful atomic bomb yet, watched on television by 35 million

15 Jun – Anne Frank's diary is published

26 Jul – Eva Peron dies of cancer, aged thirty-three

24 Aug – Kenyan Government imposes a curfew around Nairobi in an attempt to surpress the Mau Mau, a secret society committed to driving out white settlers

6 Sept – Twenty-six spectators killed in a crash at the Farnborough Air Show

3 Oct – Britain tests her first atomic bomb

19 Oct – British government to send troops to Kenya to help fight the Mau Mau

5 Nov – Eisenhower sweeps to victory in the Presidential elections

30 Nov – USA explodes the first hydrogen bomb

8 Dec – The Queen agrees to televisation of the Coronation

THE NEW QUEEN playing with Prince Charles, 4, and Princess Anne, 2, during their traditional summer break at Balmoral (left). When the King died so suddenly, Elizabeth lost not only a dearly loved father, but also the pleasures of being a young mother, free to bring up her children and enjoy a normal family life away from the public eye.

As it was, she inherited the throne and was burdened with the duties and responsibilities of sovereignty years before she might reasonably have expected. In consequence, moments such as these (below and right), when she could relax and enjoy time with her family, became more precious to her now than ever before.

THE QUEEN with Prince Charles at Balmoral (left). Although duty has kept them apart for long periods at a time, there has always been great affection between mother and son; and as heir to the throne, Charles shares with the Queen a responsibility and burden far greater than any other members of the family. They also share the fundamental loneliness of their position.

THE QUEEN delivering her first Christmas radio broadcast to Britain and the Commonwealth (right). It was a task her father, King George VI, who was afflicted by a stammer, had thoroughly disliked, so much so that the BBC devised a method of recording it in small sections. Her grandfather, George V, had always broadcast live, as did the Queen. In 1957, however, she decided to switch to the medium of television for all future Christmas broadcasts. During the summer of that year, therefore, Sylvia Peters, a BBC announcer, was filmed making a speech in a variety of poses, so that the Queen might choose how best to do it. Rather than read from a script, she opted for speaking directly to the camera, which in those days meant that her speech had to be memorized and delivered live on Christmas day.

1952 ~ 1992 ~ 1952 ~ 1992 ~ 1952 ~ 1992 ~ 1952 ~

1953

N E W S
IN BRIEF
〜

14 Jan – Josip Tito is elected President of Yugoslavia

1 Feb – 20th Century Fox announces that all of its films will now be made in wide-screen 'Cinemascope'

5 Mar – Joseph Stalin dies, aged 73

25 Mar – Queen Mary, widow of George V, dies, aged 85

25 Apr – James Watson and Francis Crick, two Cambridge scientists, discover DNA, the sequence of genetic information that makes possible all forms of biological reproduction

1 Jun – Colonel John Hunt's expedition conquers Everest

17 Jun – Soviet tanks pour into East Berlin to quell anti-Soviet protesters

25 Jun – John Christie is sentenced to hang for the murder of four women, including his wife, at 10 Rillington Place

27 Jul – An armistice is signed, ending the Korean War

19 Aug – England win the Ashes after 20 years

12 Sep – Nikita Kruschev is elected first secretary of the Communist Party in the USSR

12 Sep – Senator John F. Kennedy marries Jaqueline Bouvier

14 Nov – Londoners are issued with smog masks to combat pollution

24 Nov – US Senator McCarthy claims ex-President Truman supported many suspected Communists

10 Dec – Sir Winston Churchill is awarded the Nobel Prize for Literature

The Queen's Coronation on 2 June was a day of wonder and rejoicing, celebrated by millions of people all over the world. Hundreds of thousands of them converged on London, and every balcony, window and rooftop along the route was filled with people, hoping for a glimpse of the golden Coronation coach that made its way to Westminster Abbey.

That morning, the newspaper headlines announced that Mount Everest had been conquered for the first time in history. Commentators talked of a new Elizabethan Age, and with the end of sweet- and sugar- rationing it seemed as though Britain was well on the way to the Great Revival that was forecast.

SHIELDED BY A silken canopy, stripped of her fine robes and jewellery, Elizabeth awaits the sacred moment of her consecration (left), '. . . Be thou annointed, blessed and consecrated, Queen over the Peoples, whom the Lord thy God hath given thee to rule,' proclaimed the Archbishop of Canterbury three times. The Queen then moved to King Edward's Chair, where the Archbishop presented the tokens of sovereignty: the Orb, the Sceptre with the Cross, the Rod of Mercy, and the Royal Ring, 'the Wedding Ring of England'. Then lifting St Edward's Crown, the official Crown of England, from the altar, the Archbishop held it aloft, bringing it slowly down to rest on Elizabeth's head.

THE QUEEN in her Coronation robes (right), photographed by Beaton.

UP AND DOWN the land
people celebrated. Some
huddled round their first
black-and-white television
sets, bought specially for the
occasion. Others held giant
parties in the streets, such as
this one in Morpeth Street in
the East End of London
(above and above right), for
which the residents had been
saving up for ten months.
Everywhere people pulled
together, and recaptured
their community spirit,
something seldom seen in
the austere years since
the war.

WAVING FROM the balcony of Buckingham Palace to the cheering crowds (left). From left to right are: two Maids of Honour, the Queen, Prince Charles, Princess Anne, the Duke of Edinburgh, the Queen Mother, a lady-in-waiting, and Princess Margaret,

BRITISH PAGEANTRY at its very best. Escorted by Yeomen of the Guard, in their scarlet tights and white ruffles, the fairy-tale, gold state coach carries the Queen and the Duke of Edinburgh back to Buckingham Palace after the Coronation ceremony on 2 June (above). Despite the cold and rain, 100,000 people stood out in the street to watch the procession, which was so long it took

forty-five minutes to pass any one spot. More than 10,000 servicemen marched behind the coach. Nearly fifty bands, totalling 2,000 bandsmen, provided the music, and all along the route, guardsmen stood sentry. The details were worked out with clockwork precision by Bernard Fitzalan-Howard, sixteenth Duke of Norfolk and Hereditary Earl Marshal of England. He masterminded

the Coronation of George VI, organized three royal funerals (of George V, George VI and Queen Mary), and would later oversee the Investiture of the Prince of Wales in 1969, and Princess Anne's wedding in 1973. When statistics were finally compiled for the day, they showed that there had been 6,873 casualties, ten per cent of them serious ambulance cases. Some people had had legs broken

in the crush; others suffered exposure after spending the night on wet pavements to make sure of a good view.

1953

On a personal level, the Queen was faced with a delicate problem over her sister: Princess Margaret was in love with, and wished to marry, Group Captain Peter Townsend, DSO, DFC, who had been her father's equerry and was now Comptroller of the Queen Mother's new household at Clarence House. The family were all very fond of Townsend, but there was a very real obstacle to their marriage: Peter Townsend had been divorced.

When Margaret asked permission to marry Townsend – as the Royal Marriages Act of 1772 demanded – the Queen put it to her Prime Minister, and he in turn discussed the matter in Cabinet. Marriage, they all agreed, was unthinkable; and when the popular Press started to publicize the affair, Churchill insisted that Townsend be sent away to avoid further scandal.

CROWDS LINE the streets on 31 March to watch Queen Mary's funeral cortège making its way from Marlborough House to Westminster Hall (right). Before she died, the old Queen, who had buried three sons as well as her husband, made a point of reorganizing the catalogues of what she called 'my interesting things', so that they would be in good order when they reached her granddaughter, Elizabeth, to whom most of them were left.

GROUP CAPTAIN Peter Townsend (standing) with Princess Margaret and the Queen, watching the Olympic Horse Trials at Badminton, Gloucestershire in April (left). Bending forward (in the cap) is the Duke of Beaufort, an old friend of the family and owner of Badminton. Refused marriage to Princess Margaret later in the year, Group Captain Townsend was sent to the British Embassy in Belgium.

THE QUEEN, who stands just five feet four inches tall, is dwarfed by the soldiers of the household cavalry (below). One of Elizabeth's duties on becoming Queen was to inspect these soldiers, who act as her personal guards and who traditionally wear the familiar bearskins.

NEWS
IN BRIEF
≈

12 Feb – The British Standards Advisory Committee warns of a suspected link between smoking and lung cancer

1 Mar – The USA explodes a hydrogen bomb at Bikini Atoll in the Pacific; Japanese fishermen in a boat 70 miles away, suffer severe radiation sickness

6 May – Roger Bannister becomes the first man to break the 4-minute mile

2 Jun – Lester Piggott, aged 18, is the youngest jockey ever to win the Derby

15 Jul – The Boeing 707, the world's largest passenger plane, makes its inaugural flight

22 Jul – All rationing in Britain is ended, 14 years after its introduction

24 Aug – President Eisenhower outlaws the US Communist Party

26 Aug – *The Fellowship of the Rings*, by Oxford English professor J. R. R. Tolkien, is published

26 Oct – Colonel Nasser of Egypt survives an assassination attempt

3 Nov – Henri Matisse, French artist and leader of the Fauve group of painters, dies

30 Nov – A new portrait of Winston Churchill, by Graham Sutherland, to celebrate his 80th birthday is unveiled

2 Dec – The US Senate condemns Joseph McCarthy for conduct unbecoming to a Senator

30 Dec – The French parliament gives its approval to West German membership of NATO and re-armament

The Queen and the Duke of Edinburgh were in New Zealand for the New Year, having left Britain the previous November on a six-month tour of the Commonwealth. The couple were at last now able to visit many of the countries they had planned to go to in 1952. Elizabeth was the first reigning monarch ever to visit New Zealand; she was also the first ever to have travelled around the world, inspiring Winston Churchill to comment before her departure, 'It may well be that the journey the Queen is about to take will be no less auspicious, and the treasure she brings back no less bright, than when Drake first sailed an English ship around the world.' In the course of the tour she visited fourteen countries and covered a total of 43,618 miles, but not all by sea. Much of the journey was made by aeroplane, and in the course of it, Elizabeth became the first British monarch to fly the Atlantic.

THE QUEEN and the Duke of Edinburgh waving to a crowd of 15,000 children, in Bathurst, New South Wales (below). The royal couple were in Australia for the whole of February and March. Everywhere they went – the tour had already taken them to Bermuda, Jamaica, Panama, Fiji and Tonga, before their arrival in New Zealand two days before Christmas – they were met with a rapturous reception.

THE QUEEN and the Duke of Edinburgh inspecting the naval dockyards at Gilbraltar, with its famous rock in the background (left). It was their last port of call in a long and exhausting tour. They arrived on 10 May on the newly commissioned royal yacht *Britannia* with Prince Charles and Princess Anne, with whom they had been reunited in Malta, enabling the family to make the final leg of the journey home together.

1954

FROM AUSTRALIA the Queen and the Duke of Edinburgh flew to the Cocos Islands on 5 April, then on to Ceylon (now Sri Lanka) where they stayed for ten days. They are seen here (above) in the capital, Colombo, standing outside the Town Hall with the Mayor, Mr T. Rudra, and his wife. From Ceylon they flew to Aden, Uganda and Libya, arriving in Malta on 3 May.

1954

Prince Charles and Princess Anne were inevitably left at home with their grandmother, the Queen Mother, whilst their parents toured half the world. It was a long and painful separation for all members of the family, but in May the children flew out for a holiday with their great-uncle, Earl Mountbatten, Commander-in-Chief in the Mediterranean, who was stationed with his wife at the British Naval Base in Malta. This was very nearly the last stop on the Queen's tour, and when she and the Duke arrived in Britannia, Mountbatten put on such a daring naval manoeuvre to greet them, that the Queen, standing on Britannia's deck, was sprayed with water by some of the ships of the Fleet as they sped past, just a whisker from the royal yacht's bows.

IT SEEMED as though half of London had turned out to welcome the Queen and her family home. *Britannia* sailed up the River Thames and into the Port of London to a tumultuous reception (right). Waiting anxiously on the quayside to meet them were members of the royal family including the Queen Mother and Princess Margaret (left). They had not seen one another for almost six months.

CHARLES AND ANNE
spent most of the months
they were separated from
their parents with the Queen
Mother (top). She had looked
after her grandchildren – as
she had done so often before,
and would do again – before

they had flown out to Malta
for a short holiday with the
Mountbattens (above), while
awaiting their parents'
arrival on board *Britannia*.

The problem over Princess Margaret and Peter Townsend came to a painful end during 1955, and with it came one of the most difficult and unenviable situations of the Queen's reign. Having spent two years in Belgium, Townsend returned to London. Things had apparently changed. Margaret was now twenty-five, and under the Royal Marriages Act could marry whomever she chose. Her duty was simply to inform the Privy Council of her intention.

But in practice it was not quite so simple. Nothing had actually changed. Her sister was still Defender of the Faith, divorce was still not recognized by the Anglican Church, and their marriage would invoke serious and damaging criticism. Anthony Eden, who became Prime Minister following Churchill's resignation, told the Queen that the Cabinet strongly disapproved; one of its number, the Marquis of Salisbury, an old family friend and a High Anglican, even saw it as a resigning matter. The fact that Eden himself and three others in the Cabinet were divorced was apparently irrelevant. Margaret's duty was sadly but clearly to finish the affair, and she made a public announcement to this effect at the end of October.

THE QUEEN and the Duke of Edinburgh with Sir Winston and Lady Churchill outside Number Ten Downing Street (below), where they attended a farewell dinner on 5 April. The Prime Minister had stayed in office to see Elizabeth safely through the Coronation and her triumphant tour of the Commonwealth, but he was now over eighty and suffering from ill-health, and felt the time had come to make way for a younger man. By attending this dinner, Elizabeth became the first sovereign to be entertained in Downing Street.

THIS WORLD-FAMOUS portrait by the Italian artist Pietro Annigoni (left) was commissioned by the Fishmongers' Company in the year of the Queen's Coronation and completed in 1955. Elizabeth has spent hundreds of hours over the years sitting for portraits, most of them commissioned by regimental messes, town halls, liveried companies and high commissions. Sitting for artists is all part of the job to her.

PRINCESS MARGARET with Peter Townsend (above). On 31 October she issued a statement saying the couple would never marry. '. . . Mindful of the Church's teaching that Christian marriage is indissoluble, and conscious of my duty to the Commonwealth, I have resolved to put these considerations before any others'.

1955

1956

*T*he Queen was abroad for much of the early part of the year – visiting Nigeria, Corsica, Sardinia and Sweden – while trouble was brewing in the Middle East, culminating by the autumn in the first military confrontation of Elizabeth's reign.

The Suez Crisis was a masterpiece of diplomatic skulduggery involving Britain, France and Israel, who plotted together to oust the Egyptian President Nasser, fearing that his friendship and trade agreements with the Soviet Union and the Communist Bloc would undermine Anglo-French influence in the Middle East.

Great Britain and the USA firstly withdrew offers of financial aid to Egypt and on 26 July, after a series of tit-for-tat manoeuvres, Nasser retaliated by seizing control of the Anglo-French Suez Canal Company, which ran the all-important shipping lane. Israel then launched an attack on the Sinai region of Egypt on 29 October, and France and Britain intervened, ostensibly to stop the fighting, but also to protect their commercial interests. RAF jets began bombing Cairo on 31 October, to the immediate fury of the USA and the United Nations. The war was over in little more than a week, but its consequences raged for months.

AT THE ROYAL Film Performance on 29 October (right), the Queen meets a glamorous line-up of film stars including Marilyn Monroe, flanked by Victor Mature (to her left) and A.E. Matthews. The warmth of her smile belied the Queen's mounting concern over Suez. That same day Israel had invaded the Sinai; two days later British bombs began to fall on Cairo, and the country was at war.

KING FEISAL of Iraq is greeted by the Queen at Victoria Station, London (above), at the start of his state visit to Britain on 16 July. Just ten days later – and only six days after Feisal's departure – news reached London that his rival, President Nasser of Egypt, had seized control of the Anglo-French Suez Canal Company. When told the news, Feisal is reputed to have said, 'Get Nasser and get him now.'

THE QUEEN officially opening Calder Hall in Cumbria on 17 October (right). The first full-scale nuclear power station in the world, it provided electricity for the National Grid. Standing just behind her is the station's General Manager, Henry Davey.

THE PRIME Minister, Sir Anthony Eden, meeting the Queen at the Guildhall on 15 May (above). Although Eden claimed after the Suez débâcle later in the year that the Queen 'understood what we were doing very well', when British bombs began falling on Cairo she was said to have been surprised by the action being carried out in her name. Parliament had certainly been in the dark, as had Washington and the United Nations Security Council. But Eden was quickly forced into a cease-fire by President Eisenhower, who authorized a run on sterling by the Federal Reserve Bank and threatened Britain with ruin.

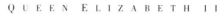

ON 8 JUNE the Queen, Princess Margaret and the Duke of Edinburgh paid a state visit to Sweden, where most of the crowned heads of Europe and their families were congregated for a festival performance at the theatre in Drottningholm, a royal castle outside Stockholm (below). Seated in the front row, from left to right, are: the Swedish Queen, Louise; Prince Bernhard of the Netherlands; Queen Elizabeth; King Gustaf Adolf of Sweden; and his daughter, Princess Josephine Charlotte.

THE QUEEN, with a cine-camera in her hand, Princess Margaret and King Gustaf Adolf of Sweden standing by one of the jumps on the cross-country course, watching the Olympic Three-Day Event which took place in Stockholm during their visit (right). Standing behind the sisters is their uncle, the Duke of Gloucester.

ON 28 JANUARY the Queen and the Duke of Edinburgh arrived in Nigeria for a tour of the largest of Britain's remaining colonial territories (left). In the course of the visit, which lasted just over two weeks and covered nearly 9,000 miles, the Queen earned high praise for visiting a leper colony on the Oji river (below). 'The Queen's visit will do more to conquer man's fear and hate of the disease than any other single act I can think of,' commented the supervisor of the colony. 'People all over the world will read that the Queen and the Duke penetrated a leper settlement and this will convince them, as nothing else could, that most of their fears of the disease are groundless.'

1957

At the beginning of the year Eden resigned, presenting Elizabeth with the task of selecting a successor. She was advised that Harold Macmillan was the Conservative Party's favourite candidate, and he duly became Prime Minister. This all took place in Prince Philip's absence: he had set off on a lengthy world tour in Britannia the previous October and was not due back until February. It was a welcome escape from the rigours of royal life that had been thrust upon him so early in his marriage, and destroyed any life of his own. Philip had found his situation very hard to accept. He had had to give up his naval career and desperately missed it, but on trips such as this he could spend time at sea, while fulfilling some of his obligations as Consort.

Philip has generally found press-reporters intrusive, irresponsible, and a terrible nuisance. In 1957 they were busy stirring rumours of a rift between him and the Queen.

The couple were clearly delighted to be together again, however. On 8 April the Queen and the Duke went on an elaborate state visit to Paris, the heart of the fashion industry, where praise for the Queen's outfits, designed by Norman Hartnell, was praise indeed.

THE DUKE of Edinburgh and the Queen, reunited in Portugal in February after 124 days apart (right). The Duke's trip on *Britannia* had aroused rumours of a rift between the couple. The Queen has seldom responded to rumours – however false – that appear in the media, but her decision to grant her husband the title of His Royal Highness the Prince Philip on his return from the South Atlantic was doubtless a way of telling the world that the rumours were false.

N E W S

IN BRIEF

≈

9 Jan – Anthony Eden resigns as Prime Minister

10 Jan – Harold Macmillan is the new Prime Minister

14 Jan – Humphrey Bogart, film star, dies of cancer, aged 56

22 Mar – The worst earthquake since 1906 hits San Francisco

25 Mar – Six nations – Belgium, France, Holland, Italy, Luxembourg and West Germany – form the Common Market

6 Jul – Althea Wilson of the USA wins the women's singles final, the first black player to win a title at Wimbledon

20 Jul – At a rally in Bradford, Macmillan tells the Party faithful that most people 'have never had it so good'

7 Aug – Oliver Hardy, fall-guy for Stan Laurel's antics, dies, aged 65

13 Sep – Agatha Christie's *The Mousetrap* enjoys its 1,998th performance, becoming Britain's longest-running play

4 Oct – The USSR launches Sputnik-I, beating the USA in the race to space

24 Oct – Christian Dior, fashion designer, dies, aged 52

3 Nov – The Soviets send a dog, Laika, into space

4 Dec – Thick fog causes a train crash at Lewisham, south London, in which 92 passengers die

25 Dec – For the first time, the Queen's Christmas Speech is broadcast on television as well as radio

THE QUEEN proudly leads her filly, Carrozza, ridden by twenty-one-year-old Lester Piggott, off the course at Epsom after their triumph in the Oaks on 7 June (left). It had been the most exciting race, which the Queen had watched with mounting tension, since the two leading horses were neck and neck to the end. A photo finish declared Carrozza the winner, and the Queen was so thrilled she made her way quickly down on to the course to lead the victorious horse in herself.

IN MID-OCTOBER the Queen and Prince Philip made a five-day state visit to the United States. On board the famous Staten Island ferry (below), President Eisenhower shows them a photograph of the famous Manhattan skyline in New York, which the royal couple compare with the original, as the ferry heads towards the mainland.

THE QUEEN reading to Princess Anne on her seventh birthday, on 15 August, in the gardens at Buckingham Palace (left). This was one of a series of delightfully informal pictures of the family taken by an unorthodox young Welsh photographer, who was making a name for himself with his unusual and dramatic photography. His work included magazine assignments and portraits, but it was in the theatrical world that he had made most impact. His striking photographs of plays and actors that hung in theatre lobbies were much talked about in the West End of London, and when the Queen wanted to commission some studies of her children, the Duchess of Kent, who was a keen theatre-goer, recommended him. His name was Antony Armstrong-Jones. Instead of the formal posed shots that previous court photographers had favoured, he asked whether he might take the children at play, then went one step further and asked the Queen to sit in shot. The resulting pictures were some of the best ever taken of the family together.

ON 23 SEPTEMBER, still hopeful that their son should have as normal an education as possible, the Queen and the Duke of Edinburgh drove a reluctant Prince Charles to begin his first term as a boarder at Cheam (left), his father's old prep school in Berkshire. For the first time in history, an heir to the throne slept in a dormitory, made his own bed, and waited at table.

PRINCE CHARLES and his father dinghy-sailing in the Solent aboard *Bluebottle* during Cowes Week in August (above). With them is the legendary designer and boat-builder Uffa Fox. The Duke, a keen yachtsman, was a regular visitor to the Isle of Wight for the annual regatta. He tried hard to enthuse the Prince in all the outdoor activities he enjoyed so much himself, but with limited success.

ACCOMPANIED by his governess, Miss Margaret Peebles, affectionately known as 'Mispy', Prince Charles arrives at Hill House, a small private day school in Knightsbridge, London, for the start of the summer term (right). Miss Peebles had been in charge of his education up until January when he had begun at the school, at the age of eight. He was to be known as Prince Charles to the staff but plain Charles to the other boys, and to be treated in every way as a normal pupil.

THE QUEEN with her mother and the Duke of Beaufort, a much-loved friend of the family, watching the Horse Trials at the Duke's Gloucestershire home, Badminton, on 18 April (above left). Badminton is one of the royal family's favourite equestrian events which the Queen attends year after year. One member often missing is the Duke of Edinburgh, who would rather be taking part in a sport than watching it. For years polo was his favourite activity, and the Queen was an avid spectator, frequently presenting the prize at the end of the day, as here at Windsor (left).

*O*n *26 July, the final day of the British Empire and Commonwealth Games in Cardiff, the Queen made an announcement:
I want to take this opportunity of speaking to all Welsh people,
not only in this arena, but wherever they may be. The British
Empire and Commonwealth Games in the capital, together
with all the activities of the Festival of Wales, have made this
a memorable year in the Principality. I have therefore decided
. . . to create my son, Charles, Prince of Wales today. When he
is grown up, I will present him to you at Caernarvon.*

*There were roars of approval from the stadium, and shouts of God
Bless the Prince of Wales, but not all Welsh people were pleased that
an English monarch was sending an English prince to rule over
them, as Charles discovered in later years. For the time being, just
nine years old and trying hard to be accepted as any other boy at
boarding-school, hearing the announcement in the headmaster's
study was simply another awkward moment.*

ON 5 DECEMBER, the
Queen made the first direct-
dial telephone call in Bristol
(opposite above right).
Previously all trunk calls
had had to go via the
operator, but with the GPO's
new system, GRACE –
group routing and charging
equipment – subscribers
could be automatically
connected to almost any
number in Britain.

THE QUEEN (left) with her
mother and sister on the
racecourse at Epsom.

GLUM EXPRESSIONS
on the faces of the Queen,
Princess Margaret and
Princess Anne (above) as
they watch the Duke of
Edinburgh's plane take off
from Heathrow Airport. The
Queen's recurring sinus-
trouble, which became so
acute that it required surgery
at the end of July, prevented
her from travelling with her
husband. While she
recuperated at home, the
Duke visited Belgium.

1958

NEWS
IN BRIEF
≈

2 Jan – Guerilla leader Fidel Castro proclaims a new government in Cuba

21 Jan – Cecil B. de Mille, film director, dies in Hollywood, aged 77

3 Feb – Buddy Holly, singer, dies in a plane crash in Iowa, aged 22

5 Feb – Australia regain the Ashes from England after five years

26 Mar – American crime novelist Raymond Chandler dies, aged 80

31 Mar – The Dalai Lama flees Tibet

9 Apr – Frank Lloyd Wright, radical American architect, dies, aged 89

28 May – Two monkeys sent on the American Jupiter missile are the first animals in space to return to earth alive

26 Jun – The Queen and President Eisenhower inaugurate the St Lawrence Seaway

18 Aug – The first photographs of Alec Issigonis' Mini car are released; the car will sell for about £500

24 Sep – Rolls Royce launch the £8,905 Phantom V

9 Oct – The Conservative Party wins a third successive General Election

14 Oct – Swashbuckling hero, Errol Flynn, dies, aged 50

27 Oct – The Queen's speech at the Opening of Parliament promises independence for Nigeria and Cyprus

19 Nov – The Government announces that the Bank of England will re-introduce £10 notes for the first time since the War

*P*rince Philip set off once again on a lengthy tour, leaving the Queen at home with the children. She had suffered badly with sinus-trouble towards the end of the previous year, and her health was not yet one hundred per cent.

She also had an extensive tour of Canada and the United States coming up in June, and was preserving her strength. Shortly before leaving, Elizabeth discovered she was pregnant, but insisted upon going ahead with the tour none the less. Battling against intense heat, she embarked on a strenuous schedule.

At home, Princess Margaret had fallen in love with Antony Armstrong-Jones, the photographer who had taken such charming pictures of the Queen and her family two years earlier to commemorate Princess Anne's seventh birthday.

MOTHER AND daughter with some of their best friends (below). The Queen has been surrounded by horses and dogs ever since she was a little girl. She began riding at the age of two and a half, at three was given her first pony, and never looked back. Anne also had her first pony at three, and Mayflower, pictured here, was her third.

PRESIDENT DWIGHT Eisenhower and the Queen at the official opening of the St Lawrence Seaway in Canada in June (above). Afterwards, building on the relationship she had formed with the American President during her trip to the United States two years earlier, she and the Duke of Edinburgh entertained the Eisenhowers on board *Britannia*. For someone in the early stages of pregnancy, the tour comprised a strenuous schedule, being undertaken much of the time in intense heat. As well as the usual banquets and receptions, and visits to factories and hospitals, she took a trip down an open-pit iron mine at Knob Lake, Quebec. During the visit she met some of the men who worked the mine (right). By the time she returned home, six weeks and 17,633 miles later, she was exhausted and her doctors insisted that she must rest.

THE QUEEN with Sir Anthony Blunt (above) at the Courtauld Institute of Art in London, of which he was Director. Anthony Blunt, to whom she awarded the KCVO in 1956, had been Surveyor of the Queen's Pictures since the beginning of Elizabeth's reign, and of her father's since 1945. Throughout this time, Blunt had been a Russian spy, as Margaret Thatcher, the Prime Minister, admitted to the House of Commons in 1979. Blunt confessed to being a spy to British Intelligence in 1964, but no action was subsequently taken because his role within the royal household 'carried with it no access to classified information and no risk to security'.

The Prime Minister, Harold Macmillan, began the year with an extensive tour of Africa, trailing controversy in his wake as he warned white South African politicians that 'there is a wind of change blowing through this continent. . . .' Elizabeth's mind, however, was on more personal matters, and the birth of Prince Andrew on 19 February brought immense happiness.

Shortly before Andrew's birth, the Queen announced a change in the family surname. 'While I and my family shall continue to be styled and known as the House of Windsor,' she said, 'my descendants . . . shall bear the name Mountbatten-Windsor.' Her decision was motivated by a desire to associate her husband's name with their descendants. There is no doubt Philip was delighted, as was his uncle, Lord Mountbatten, who had been trying to include the family name in the royal surname for years.

A week after Andrew's birth, Princess Margaret announced her engagement to Antony Armstrong-Jones. Their wedding on 6 May was a glorious occasion and a huge celebration, with people once again sleeping overnight in the Mall to secure a good view.

A DELIGHTED family admire the new addition (below). His excited sister was able to have a look at Prince Andrew within an hour of his birth on 19 February, but Charles, away at Cheam, had to wait longer. He was playing the part of Richard III in a school play when the headmaster interrupted the performance to announce that the Queen had given birth to another son.

THE QUEEN, the Queen Mother and Prince Charles make the journey by coach along flag-strewn streets and excited crowds to Westminster Abbey for Princess Margaret's wedding to Antony Armstrong-Jones on 6 May (below). No two women could have been more delighted, and relieved, that after all her heartache Margaret at last seemed to have found happiness and love.

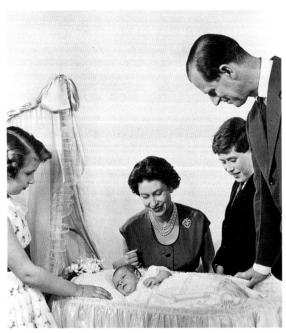

PRINCESS MARGARET in the Throne Room at Buckingham Palace after her wedding on 6 May (left). The dress, specially created for her by Norman Hartnell, used thirty yards of white silk organza; it was designed to represent the portraits of angels in medieval paintings, and the effect was stunning. Attended by eight bridesmaids, including Princess Anne, Margaret looked simply beautiful, and the nation felt uplifted. The wedding was the first major ceremonial royal day since the Queen's Coronation, and was cause for great celebration, with bunting and flowers strewn from windows and lamp-posts, and people turning out in their thousands to watch and feel part of the occasion. The weather was perfect. The glass coach sparkled in the sunshine as the Princess – accompanied by the Duke of Edinburgh, who gave her away – rode to Westminster Abbey, waving happily to the crowds. After the marriage ceremony, the newly-weds (above, in an official engagement picture) were cheered all the way back to Buckingham Palace. Later, as they boarded *Britannia* for a honeymoon in the Caribbean, they were sent on their way with a chorus of ships' sirens, church bells, cheers, whistles and hooters.

1960

ON 5 APRIL, less than
two months after giving birth
to Prince Andrew, the Queen
was back on public duty
(right), welcoming the
French President, Charles
de Gaulle, to Britain at the
start of his first state visit
since coming to power.

THE COMMONWEALTH
Prime Ministers' Conference
at Windsor Castle on 2 May
(below) was specifically
timed to coincide with
Princess Margaret's
wedding, to which the prime
ministers were invited.

NEWS
IN BRIEF
≈

4 Jan – French intellectual and existentialist writer, Albert Camus, is killed in a car crash, aged 46

24 Jan – Pope John XXIII warns Catholics of the dangers of many films and television programmes

21 Mar – South African police shoot dead 56 people in the black township of Sharpeville

9 Apr – A white South African fires two shots at and injures the South African Prime Minister, Dr Verwoerd

5 May – The USSR shoots down a US U-2 plane, piloted by Francis Gary Powers, claiming it was on a spying mission

30 Jun – The Congo gains independence from Belgium

21 Jul – Francis Chichester completes his solo crossing of the Atlantic in record time

21 Jul – Mrs Sirimavo Bandaranaike of Ceylon is sworn in as the world's first woman prime minister

1 Oct – Nigeria, Britain's biggest colony, gains independence

10 Nov – Penguin Books publishes *Lady Chatterley's Lover*, the Old Bailey having ruled it is not obscene; the first print run of 200,000 copies sells out on the first day

16 Nov – Clark Gable, Hollywood legend, dies, aged 59

9 Nov – John F. Kennedy wins the US Presidential election, the youngest man, at 43, ever to do so

31 Dec – The army calls up the last men who will be required for National Service

1960

THE QUEEN with Harold Macmillan, dressed in his robes as Chancellor of Oxford University and welcoming her during an official visit. They had built up a warm relationship during his three years as Prime Minister, and shared similar views on a number of issues. Macmillan had done much to mend the damage done to Britain's relationship with President Eisenhower over Suez, and the Queen supported him in his view that the safety of Britain lay in a unified stand with the United States against the Soviet Union.

ON 21 OCTOBER the Queen launched the Navy's first nuclear-powered submarine, HMS *Dreadnought* (below). Lord Mountbatten had secured American co-operation with the project. He saw great potential in nuclear power. 'There are glittering prizes to be won,' he said, 'not least by making our merchant ships less dependent on that controversial commodity, oil.'

THE QUEEN and the Duke of Edinburgh with the new American President, John F. Kennedy and his glamorous wife, Jackie (below), at Buckingham Palace in June. Kennedy had come to Britain from Vienna, where, in a move to improve East-West relations, he had met the Soviet President, Nikita Khrushchev, with little success: two months later, the Berlin Wall was erected.

The Queen and the Duke of Edinburgh were abroad for several months of the year, beginning in January with a tour of India. They returned home to the news that Princess Margaret was expecting a baby. Antony Armstrong-Jones had not wanted to be given a title when he married Princess Margaret, but he was persuaded that, for the sake of his children, who would be in line to the throne, he should now accept. At the end of the summer he was created the Earl of Snowdon, and when Margaret gave birth to a son, David, he was titled Viscount Linley.

On 9 November the Queen travelled to Ghana. There had been violent civil unrest in the country and threats against the life of the President, Dr Kwame Nkrumah. But despite advice that she should cancel the visit, the Queen insisted on going.

QUEEN ELIZABETH II

1961

IT WAS A HISTORIC occasion when the Queen was greeted by the Pope at his palace in the Vatican City (above), the first time ever that the heads of the Church of England and the Catholic Church had met in Rome.

PROUD PARENTS, Princess Margaret and Lord Snowdon travel home with their new-born baby son, David (left).

IN JANUARY the Queen and the Duke of Edinburgh were guests of President Jawaharlal Nehru, during Elizabeth's first visit to India. She enjoys a polo match with him (right), and (below) hosts a garden party at the British High Commission in Delhi. But what caught the attention of the world, and caused considerable consternation, was their participation in a tiger hunt with the Maharajah of Jaipur (far right), organized by the famous big-game hunter, Colonel Keshari Singh. Wildlife conservationists and animal-lovers were outraged, and sent letters and telegrams of disgust. The Duke, to make matters worse, had shot a male tiger.

1962

On 11 May, Prince Charles was sent away to his father's old school, Gordonstoun, a desolate, spartan institute in the north of Scotland. Founded by the German educationalist, Kurt Hahn, the regime was tough, and lived up to school's motto Plus est en vous ('There is more in you'). If the boys weren't out running half-naked in mid-winter, as they had to do before a cold shower and breakfast every morning, they were sailing in the icy North Sea, or climbing down cliff ladders. Charles felt very isolated, despite visits from his grandmother from time to time.

At large, the launch of Private Eye, the satirical magazine, and the start of television's irreverent satirical programme, That Was The Week That Was, showed that those in power were beginning to lose their mystique. Unnerved by disastrous by-election results and charges that there was no national leadership, on 13 July – dubbed 'the night of the long knives' after Adolf Hitler's purge of the SA in 1934 – Macmillan informed the Queen that he was sacking seven members of his Cabinet.

PRINCE CHARLES (below), newly arrived at Gordonstoun on 11 May, meets Peter Paice (centre), the head of school, and Dougal McKenzie, the head of his house, Windmill Lodge. Both boys are wearing the school uniform of open-necked shirt and short trousers with no pockets. It was a harsh environment, and for the first two years Charles was bitterly unhappy there.

THE QUEEN and the Bishop of Coventry on the steps of the new Coventry Cathedral (right) after its consecration on 25 May. Behind them is Epstein's statue of St Michael and the Devil. The ultra-modern building replaced the original Cathedral, bombed during the war, and aroused considerable controversy.

THE QUEEN looking much cheered by an evening spent watching a Gang Show in Golders Green, London, on 28 November (below).

4 Jan – President Kennedy promises further military aid to the government of South Vietnam

26 Jan – Salvatore 'Lucky' Luciano, head of the mafia in the USA, dies of a heart attack

4 Feb – Britain's first colour magazine supplement goes out with the *Sunday Times*

10 Feb – The USA swaps KGB Colonel Rudolph Abel for Gary Powers

2 Apr – The first push-button 'panda' crossings are introduced to Britain

30 Apr – *Private Eye* is launched

25 Jun – Sophia Loren, the Italian film star, is charged with bigamy

3 Jul – France declares the independence of Algeria

25 Jul – Civil war breaks out in Algeria

5 Aug – Norma Jean Baker, aka Marilyn Monroe, dies of a drug overdose

1 Oct – James Meredith's first day as Mississippi University's first black student provokes riots

15 Oct – Amnesty International is founded

28 Oct – President Kruschev promises to dismantle Soviet missiles based in Cuba in return for America lifting the naval blockade of the island

24 Nov – *That Was The Week That Was* starts broadcasting

29 Nov – Britain and France sign an agreement to develop and build a supersonic aeroplane

6 Dec – The latest 'wave' of London smog has killed 60 people in three days

*A*t the end of January the Queen and Prince Philip left for a
tour, visiting Fiji, New Zealand, Australia and Canada,
clocking up a total of 42,062 miles in two months. On their return
to England they found the Government on the brink of crisis. John
Profumo, the Secretary of State for War, the man in charge of
steering the Government's nuclear, anti-Soviet policy, stood accused
of having had an affair, two years earlier, with a prostitute name
Christine Keeler, who had sold her story to the Sunday Pictorial.
Another of her bedfellows had been a Russian naval attaché,
Captain Yevgeny Ivanov. Although the offical inquiry found that
Profumo had posed no security risk, his political career was
finished. Macmillan's handling of the affair was strongly criticized:
in October, in failing health, the Prime Minister resigned.

DRESSED IN protective clothing, the Queen is clearly enjoying a visit on 13 March to a hydro-electric scheme in the Snowy Mountains in Australia (below). She was driven two miles into a tunnel being bored into the mountains, and was cheered long and loud by more than 200 workers at the rock face.

ELIZABETH in her role as Queen of New Zealand, and dressed for the part, at the opening of the New Zealand Parliament in Wellington, on 12 February (below). Walking down the steps by her side is the Prime Minister, Keith Holyoake, and behind her follows the Duke of Edinburgh.

HER SKIRT caught by a sudden gust of wind, the Queen battles to maintain her dignity (above). She and the Duke of Edinburgh had just arrived at a new estate on the outskirts of Wellington during their two-week visit to New Zealand.

THE QUEEN and the Duke of Edinburgh (right) dressed in the ancient ceremonial robes worn by Knights of the Order of the Thistle, at St Giles's Cathedral in Edinburgh on 2 July. The Thistle is one of four main orders of knighthood in Great Britain. These date back to the Middle Ages, once being recognition for military prowess, but now a general honour. The other Orders are the Garter, the Bath, and the St Patrick; all non-hereditary titles, and each bestowed in a special ceremony each year.

IT WAS A warm welcome, as always, that greeted the arrival of the Queen and the Duke of Edinburgh in February when they spent two days in Fiji *en route* to New Zealand (above).

ON 9 JULY, the Queen and King Paul I of Greece (right) make the short journey from Victoria Station to Buckingham Palace at the start of a controversial state visit with his wife, Queen Frederike. There was tight security throughout their stay for fear of assassination attempts, after the murder in Athens of a leading nuclear disarmament supporter. Angry demonstrators hounded the couple, waving placards, and shouting 'Nazi' and 'Sieg Heil', in reference to the number of political prisoners in Greek gaols.

KING BAUDOUIN of Belgium had proved a more welcome visitor when he arrived in London for a three-day visit on 14 May, accompanied by his wife, Queen Fabiola. It was a relaxed party that arrived at Covent Garden for an evening at the opera (right).

NEWS
IN BRIEF

≈

15 Jan – The BBC ends its ban on mentioning politics, royalty, religion and sex in comedies

14 Feb – Harold Wilson is elected leader of the Labour Party

5 Jun – John Profumo resigns from the Cabinet, and admits he lied when he denied any impropriety in his relationship with Christine Keeler

16 Jun – Russian Lieutenant Valentina Tereshkova is the first woman in space

1 Jul – MPs are told that 'Kim' Philby was the 'third man', who tipped off spies Burgess and Maclean

3 Jul – The Government announces the introduction of continental road signs to Britain

31 Jul – Stephen Ward, on trial for living on immoral earnings, takes an overdose; he dies on 3 August

8 Aug – The 'Great Train Robbery' nets robbers more than £1 million

28 Aug – Martin Luther King tells a crowd of 200,000 'I have a dream . . .' at a civil rights rally in Washington

10 Sep – American Express launches its credit card in Britain

10 Oct – Macmillan resigns as Prime Minister; he is replaced by Alec Home

31 Oct – Sales of 'She Loves You' by the Beatles top one million

22 Nov – John F. Kennedy, 43rd President of the USA, is shot dead in Dallas, Texas, aged 46

24 Nov – Lee Harvey Oswald, charged with the assassination of President Kennedy, is murdered by Jack Ruby, a strip-club owner

12 Dec – Kenya gains independence from Britain

ON 24 APRIL, the marriage of Princess Alexandra of Kent to Angus Ogilvy in Westminster Abbey was another day of magnificent pomp and pageantry, attended by all the royal family (left). Like Margaret, the Queen's cousin had chosen to marry a commoner – a businessman – and he too had turned down any offer of a title. He resolutely remained a private individual and continued with his business career, taking the view, as Antony Armstrong-Jones had done, that he was not a member of the royal family, he was simply married to one.

AFTER THE MISERY Prince Charles suffered when he first went to school, the Queen looks somewhat apprehensive as she delivers Princess Anne to Benenden, near Cranbrook in Kent, in September (right). She need not have worried; her robust only daughter, happily greeting Elizabeth Somershield, assigned to show her the ropes, and head girl, Mary Anne Southby, took to boarding quite cheerfully. Like Charles, she was accompanied by a detective who lived in the school grounds.

The birth of her fourth child, Edward, on 10 March forced the Queen to adopt a relatively low profile for the first half of the year – limiting her public engagements to events such as Trooping the Colour – as she concentrated on family matters and regained her strength.

Elsewhere, however, life was not so calm, as the Queen soon found out. In early October she left for a tour of Canada amid assassination threats from militant separatists. In Quebec, extremists bedecked with hostile placards turned their backs on the royal motorcade as it passed by, and when the Queen arrived at the Legislative Building angry demonstrators shouted, booed, and waved banners claiming 'Quebec for the Quebecois'. Alarming as it was, the Queen showed no outward signs of distress, and continued her official programme as planned, carrying out her engagements with customary dignity.

She and the Duke of Edinburgh arrived back in Britain the day before the General Election on 15 October, which resulted in the first Labour victory of Elizabeth's reign and the Party's return to government after thirteen years of Tory rule. The following day Harold Wilson arrived at Buckingham Palace for his audience with the Queen, accompanied not only by his wife, but by his father and sister, too, who were not received by the Queen but smartly ushered into an equerry's office. Wilson could not have struck a more contrasting figure to his predecessor, the lean and aristocratic Sir Alec Douglas-Home, but over the weeks the Queen warmed to her new Prime Minister, who knew little about royal etiquette and was surprised to discover just how thoroughly the sovereign read her 'boxes' in preparation for their weekly meetings.

It was a bumper year for royal babies: as well as Prince Edward's birth, Princess Margaret had a daughter, Lady Sarah Armstrong-Jones, whilst the Duchess of Kent also gave birth to a daughter, Lady Helen Windsor.

ON 10 MARCH, at the age of thirty-seven, the Queen gave birth to another son, Prince Edward (opposite below). She could not have been more delighted. Her family was now complete and she was determined to enjoy her last baby to the full. The rest of the family, gathered round his pram in the garden at Buckingham Palace (left), were also delighted. Prince Charles and Princess Anne, both away at school when he was born, had to wait for the Easter holidays before they saw their new brother, but four-year-old Prince Andrew was at home, and his father took him to see the new arrival straight away. Although there had been no complications, the Queen was tired after the delivery, and her doctors advised a rest, but by the Trooping the Colour, her official birthday in June, she was back on form, proudly showing off her new son to the world (opposite above).

NEWS
IN BRIEF
≈

25 Feb – Cassius Clay wins the world heavyweight boxing championship

15 Mar – Actors Richard Burton and Elizabeth Taylor marry

27 Mar – Ten men are found guilty of the Great Train Robbery

13 Apr – Ian Smith is elected Prime Minister of Rhodesia

21 Apr – BBC2 begins transmission; the first programme shown is *Play School*

18 May – Mods and Rockers clash at seaside resorts

28 May – Jawaharlal Nehru, Prime Minister of India since independence in 1947, dies

14 Jun – Nelson Mandela is found guilty of treason and is sentenced to life imprisonment

2 Jul – President Lyndon Johnson signs the Civil Rights Act, outlawing racial discrimination in the USA

6 Jul – Princess Margaret attends the premiere of the Beatles film *A Hard Day's Night* in London

7 Aug – The USA prepares to step up action against the Communist forces of North Vietnam

4 Sep – The Forth Bridge, the longest in Europe, is opened

15 Sep – The *Daily Herald* newspaper is relaunched as the *Sun*

15 Oct – Kruschev is deposed as leader of the USSR and replaced by Leonid Brezhnev

16 Oct – Harold Wilson's Labour Party wins the General Election after 13 years of Conservative rule

24 Oct – Martin Luther King is awarded the Nobel Prize for Peace

21 Dec – MPs vote to abolish the death penalty

SITTING before a packed House of Lords for the State Opening of Parliament on 3 November (opposite), the Queen announces her Government's legislative and political agenda for the forthcoming session.

ENJOYMENT shows on the Queen's face as she hosts a dinner at Buckingham Palace for Commonwealth prime ministers (above), on the eve of their London Conference in July.

THE QUEEN shakes hands with Harold Wilson (left), her first Labour Prime Minister, at a reception at County Hall in London.

1965

*O*n 24 January Sir Winston Churchill died at the age of ninety. The Queen was deeply saddened by the loss of this giant of a man whom she had known since childhood, and who had helped, guided and advised her with such fatherly affection through the early years of her reign. To the vast majority of British people he was mourned as the greatest statesman of the twentieth century – the man who had steered the country through the Second World War – and the nation grieved. For three days his body lay in state in Westminster Abbey, where 130,000 people, including the Queen, came silently to pay their last respects. By solemn military procession, his coffin was then taken to St Paul's Cathedral, where he was afforded the honour of a full state funeral, attended by representatives of more than one hundred nations. It was one of the rare occasions when the Queen has attended the funeral of a commoner. Afterwards his body was taken up the River Thames to Waterloo station, and on to Oxfordshire, where he was buried in the village churchyard at Bladon, near his ancestral home of Blenheim.

DEFYING THE wet and windy weather, ordinary people turned out in their thousands on 30 January, lining the streets and crowding on to balconies (below), to say a final farewell to Sir Winston Churchill, bowing their heads as the coffin of the great wartime hero – the man who had saved them from the clutches of Adolf Hitler – passed by.

THE FUNERAL cortège (left) makes its way solemnly from Westminster Abbey to St Paul's Cathedral, where the Queen and the Duke of Edinburgh stand in the bitter cold to meet it (below). Drums thundered outside as the pallbearers laid the coffin down on Wren's memorial inscription; the 'Battle Hymn of the Republic' was played in honour of Churchill's American mother; then, in the silence that followed, a trumpeter in a medieval tunic sounded the chilling notes of the Last Post from the Whispering Gallery.

ON 10 AUGUST, the Queen, accompanied by the Duke of Edinburgh, inspects HMS *Dido* during her review of the Home Fleet in the Clyde (below). Also in the party is Earl Mountbatten, who had recently retired as First Sea Lord and Chief of Defence Staff.

THE QUEEN leaving Yarmouth on the Isle of Wight to make her first journey by hovercraft on 27 July (right). The first of these noisy sea-buses came into public service in 1959, making short-haul trips in fair weather only. This larger, more robust model was undergoing trials prior to the inauguration of a cross-Channel service the following year.

NEWS
IN BRIEF

≈

4 Jan – T. S. Eliot, Modernist poet, dies, aged 77

24 Jan – Sir Winston Churchill, dies, aged 90

8 Feb – Cigarette advertising is banned from British television

11 Feb – Ringo Starr marries Maureen Cox

21 Feb – Radical black Moslem, Malcolm X, is shot dead

18 Mar – Cosmonaut Alexei Leonev is the first man to walk in space

31 Mar – The USA sends marines to Vietnam, the first American fighting soldiers to be committed to the war

6 Apr – Julie Andrews wins an Oscar for *Mary Poppins*

1 May – Liverpool win the FA Cup for the first time in the club's history

11 Jun – The Beatles are awarded MBEs in the Honours List

27 Jul – Edward Heath is elected leader of the Conservative Party

18 Aug – David Bailey marries Catherine Deneuve

27 Aug – Le Corbusier, Modernist architect, dies, aged 77

7 Oct – The Queen opens the Post Office Tower

28 Oct – Ian Brady and Myra Hindley are charged with the murder of Lesley Anne Downey whose body was found on Saddleworth Moor

11 Nov – Ian Smith, Rhodesia's Prime Minister, issues a Unilateral Declaration of Independence from Britain

15 Dec – Goldie the eagle escapes from London Zoo, the second time in a year

LIKE MOTHER, like daughter. The Queen and Princess Anne in rapt concentration (above) as they watch a competitor ride the cross-country course at Badminton Horse Trials in April. The Queen is wearing a headscarf that is her trademark on these informal equestrian occasions. The camera slung round her neck is another of the familiar props she is seldom without.

DRESSED in an evening gown, fur stole and diamond tiara (right), the Queen arrives at a Gala Performance of *Hello Dolly*, accompanied by the Archbishop of Canterbury, Dr Michael Ramsay, a friend and adviser. Later in the year, shortly before Christmas, he was one of a group of wise men invited to Windsor Castle to discuss Prince Charles's future after Gordonstoun. The others included Harold Wilson, Sir Charles Wilson (chairman of the Committee of University Vice-Chancellors) and Lord Mountbatten.

THE FAMILY together at the Braemar Games (above), a traditional port of call every year that takes place in the midst of their summer holiday in the Highlands of Scotland. Pictured from left to right are: Prince Philip, the Queen, the Queen Mother, Prince Charles, Princess Anne, Princess Margaret and Lord Snowdon.

ON 18 MAY, the Queen and the Duke of Edinburgh embarked on a tricky ten-day state visit to West Germany, the first such visit since the Second World War. The British Press were subdued about the trip, but the *Sunday Times* saw it as 'a sign that this country has at last realigned its views about the Germans and accepts them genuinely as allies and human beings.' The Queen smiled cheerfully in Munich (below), and, addressing a banquet in Bonn, hosted by the President, Heinrich Lukhe, she spoke of uniting Europe on 'as broad a base as possible'. But a visit to the Berlin Wall (right), constructed four years earlier, was a reminder of the realities of the Cold War.

IN FEBRUARY the Queen and Prince Philip paid their first state visit to Ethiopia (left) as guests of Emperor Haile Selassie whose grand-children, Princess Mary and Princess Sahine, were fellow pupils of Princess Anne's at Benenden. After a week in Ethiopia, the couple flew to Sudan for five days before parting company. The Queen returned home, while the Prince set off on a tour of the Orient and Australia.

1952 ~ 1992 ~

1965

*I*n February, the Duke of Windsor was admitted to the London
Clinic for an eye operation, accompanied by the Duchess. The
Queen had long felt that the time had come to offer some gesture of
friendship, but she had always held back out of loyalty to her
mother, who had never been able to forgive the couple for forcing the
stress of kingship upon her husband. After consulting her mother,
the Queen went to visit her uncle at the Clinic, the first time they
had met in twenty-nine years. The Duke requested that when he died
he be buried in the family burial ground at Frogmore; and that
when the Duchess died, she might be permitted to lie alongside him.
The Queen granted the request.

HAROLD MACMILLAN
speaking, on 14 May, at the
dedication ceremony at
Runnymede of a memorial to
the assassinated American
President, John F. Kennedy,
shot dead in November
1963. In the front row are:
Prince Philip, the Queen,
and JFK's widow, Jackie
Kennedy. Behind Jackie are
her daughter, Caroline, and
Robert F. Kennedy. Senator
Edward Kennedy and his
wife, Joan, are seated
behind Macmillan.

1966

Shortly after seeing Prince Charles off to spend six months in the Australian bush at Timbertop, the Queen and the Duke of Edinburgh left for an extensive tour of the Caribbean at the beginning of February. They arrived home in time for a General Election which saw Harold Wilson returned to power with an increased Labour majority; and the problem of Rhodesia still to solve, where rebel Prime Minister Ian Smith had illegally declared the country independent from the Commonwealth the previous November. The Queen had been closely involved in trying to avert UDI, and was firmly behind Wilson in his decision to use economic sanctions rather than military force to redress the situation.

THE QUEEN with some Yeomen of the Guard, more commonly known as Beefeaters, during an inspection on 7 June (left). No more than a hundred in number, they are a body of foot guards, established during the reign of Henry VII for the sovereign's personal protection. They still wear the style of uniform worn by their predecessors in Tudor times, and their duties nowadays are clearly delineated. They must be present on ceremonial state occasions, they must attend the yearly distribution of Maundy money, and they must search the vaults of the Houses of Parliament on 5 November, Guy Fawkes Day, each year.

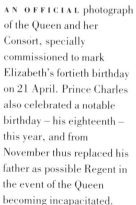

AN OFFICIAL photograph of the Queen and her Consort, specially commissioned to mark Elizabeth's fortieth birthday on 21 April. Prince Charles also celebrated a notable birthday – his eighteenth – this year, and from November thus replaced his father as possible Regent in the event of the Queen becoming incapacitated.

PRINCESS ALICE of Greece (right) the Duke of Edinburgh's eighty-one-year-old mother, and Mother Superior of a religious Order of nuns. In February, Prince Philip – worried for her safety in Athens – had tried to persuade her to come and live in England. The following year she accepted, moving to Buckingham Palace, where she remained until her death in 1969.

THERE WAS national euphoria on 30 July when England won the World Cup. The Queen, not noted as a football fan, was at Wembley to see their triumphant 4–2 win over West Germany in the final. Germany were first to score in the match, but Geoff Hurst equalized and then Martin Peters scored to take England into the lead. A last-minute goal by Germany took the match into extra time, but two more goals by Hurst were enough to secure England's victory. The Queen was clearly delighted, as can be seen when she presented the Cup to England's captain, Bobby Moore (above).

ON 21 OCTOBER disaster struck the small South Wales mining village of Aberfan. A mountainous coal tip collapsed in the middle of the day, engulfing the primary school and killing 144 people, of whom 116 were children. The enormity of the tragedy shocked the nation, and the Queen's visit to the site, where she met grieving parents and bewildered survivors, was one of the most moving moments of her reign. She and the Duke of Edinburgh placed a wreath on the mass grave (above), already strewn with flowers, and they spoke to eight-year-old Alison Lewis (above right), who was rescued from the rubble.

IN POIGNANT contrast, the Queen visited the Rivers County Infant School, in Bletchley, Buckinghamshire, on 4 April (left). The children are so engrossed in their painting they scarcely notice their royal visitor.

IGNORING THREATS of violence, the Queen made a two-day visit to Northern Ireland at the beginning of July, arriving by helicopter (below), one of her least favourite modes of transport. Security was very tight and it was a tense trip: she passed angry demonstrations, a youth threw a concrete block in her direction as she drove through the streets, and a young woman threw a bottle which actually hit the car window. But there were quieter moments, too, such as a luncheon (left), where she sips a cup of coffee at the end of the meal.

1967
~ 1992 ~
~ 1952 ~
~ 1952 ~

The unveiling of a plaque to commemorate the centenary of Queen Mary's birth was the excuse for a public reconciliation with the Duke and Duchess of Windsor. As Queen Mary's eldest son, the Duke was an important guest, although ironically it was she who had so adamantly blocked the Duchess being accorded the title Her Royal Highness. Thus in June the Windsors arrived in England – and for the first time in over thirty years their visit was by invitation of the Queen. The ice was broken, and thereafter, although she did not visit herself, the Queen positively encouraged younger members of the family to visit the Windsors in France.

In October Prince Charles arrived at Trinity College, Cambridge, following in his grandfather's footsteps. But unlike George VI, he attended as a normal student, much to his obvious enjoyment.

At the end of the year, the military junta *in Greece that had deposed King Constantine in April uncovered plans for a counter-coup and so drove the King, his wife, Queen Frederike (his mother), and Princess Andrew (Prince Philip's elderly mother, Alice) into exile. At the Queen and Prince Philip's insistence, Princess Andrew came to live at Buckingham Palace.*

THE DUKE and Duchess of Windsor arrive in Britain on 7 June for the unveiling of Queen Mary's commemorative plaque (below). They were met by Lord Mountbatten and spent their first night at Broadlands, before moving to Claridge's hotel in London. The Court Circular made no mention of their arrival nor of their presence at the ceremony.

A STUDY OF Elizabeth taken by the Canadian portrait photographer Yousuf Karsh (opposite).

THE QUEEN warmly welcoming King Faisal of Saudi Arabia for an eight-day state visit to Britain on 9 May (below). One of the Queen's most valuable roles is in forging friendships with foreign leaders, which are beneficial in terms of trade and also in maintaining stable political alliances.

NEWS
IN BRIEF

≈

4 Jan – Donald Campbell dies while attempting to break the world water speed record

16 Jan – The last-ever issue of *Boys' Own* magazine is published

27 Jan – Three American astronauts die when fire guts their Apollo spacecraft during a launch rehearsal

30 Mar – The *Torrey Canyon* oil tanker is wrecked off the coast of Cornwall

30 Apr – Muhammed Ali is stripped of his world heavyweight title for refusing the military draft

1 Jun – The Beatles release *Sergeant Pepper's Lonely Hearts Club Band*

27 Jun – Barclays Bank introduces automatic cash dispensers

10 Jun – Spencer Tracy, movie star, dies, aged 67

10 Jun – Israel agrees to a ceasfire after a six-day war with Arab states

1 Jul – BBC2 begins regular colour broadcasts

14 Jul – Parliament passes a bill to legalize abortions in Britain

16 Jul – Hyde Park plays host to a massive 'legalize pot' rally

8 Oct – Prince Charles starts his first term at Cambridge University

9 Oct – Che Guevara, revolutionary and guerilla, is shot dead, aged 39

19 Nov – The Labour Government devalues sterling

21 Nov – The USA steps up bomb attacks against North Vietnam

1 Dec – Britain's first black headmaster starts work

3 Dec – The world's first successful human heart transplant is carried out in Cape Town, South Africa

ROUND-THE-WORLD, solo yachtsman, Francis Chichester, aged sixty-six, goes down on one knee (left) as he is knighted by the Queen at the Royal Naval College in Greenwich on 7 July. Six weeks earlier, on 28 May, he had sailed into Portsmouth, to a rapturous reception, in his small boat, *Gypsy Moth IV*, having been at sea for 226 days. He had sailed from Portsmouth to Sydney and back, a total of 29,600 miles, the fastest true circumnavigation port to port by any small boat.

THE QUEEN keeps a healthy distance when introduced to Rabiu the cheetah during a visit to the London Zoo on 16 May (left). While she was there she took the opportunity to visit the Zoo's recently opened avant-garde Aviary. Designed by her brother-in-law, Lord Snowdon, the Aviary was the first major construction to have been built at the Zoo since the famous Modernist Penguin Pool in 1936, and was part of a major re-building scheme that included a new Elephant and Rhino Pavilion and, in the Seventies, a Primate House and Lion Terraces.

JAMES BOND star, Sean Connery, meets the Queen at the London première of *You Only Live Twice* on 12 June (left). To Connery's right are his wife, actress Diane Cilento, and American comedian Dick van Dyke. The Queen was a great fan of the Bond films, and one of Prince Andrew's most prized possessions was a scale-model of 007's Aston Martin, a gift from the film makers.

THE QUEEN and the Duke of Edinburgh wave enthusiastically (below left) as they watch the launching of the celebrated new liner, *Queen Elizabeth II*, on 20 September.

THE QUEEN meets members of the England cricket team (below). Standing behind her is the England Captain, Brian Close. The Queen watches at least one Test match during the season, and during the tea-break goes on to the pitch to meet the members of both teams. One year, the Australian cricketer, Dennis Lilley, pulled a photograph out of his pocket and asked her to sign it for his 'mates back home'. The Queen laughingly declined – she never gives autographs – but subsequently sent him a signed picture of herself.

1968

Ugly racial tension marred much of the year in Britain, and brought demonstrators to the gates of Buckingham Palace calling for a ban on immigration by 'Negroes and coloureds'. The explosive reaction was sparked off by Enoch Powell, the Conservative MP, whose 'rivers of blood' speech in Birmingham on 21 April predicted racial violence on the streets unless immigration was controlled. Morale was at an all-time low in the country. And to add to the Queen's unease, there was civil war in Nigeria.

On a personal level, things were not much better. In August, Princess Marina, a much-loved aunt, died of a brain tumour. Welsh nationalists were issuing threats against Prince Charles and were promising violence at his investiture as Prince of Wales planned for the following year.

THE QUEEN chatting to members of the Royal Forestry Society in Windsor Great Park on 5 May (right). As owner of some of the greatest tracts of forestry in the country, it is a subject she has more than a passing interest in.

SURROUNDED by her family, the Queen, at forty-two, sits in the spring sunshine in the gardens at Windsor Castle (left). Prince Charles, at nineteen, was enjoying the freedom of life at university, reading archaeology and anthropology. He later changed to history. Princess Anne, aged seventeen, was still at Benenden preparing to take two 'A' levels in June. Like Charles, she had recently begun to take part in state occasions, such as the Opening of Parliament and the Queen's garden parties. The two little ones, Prince Andrew, eight, and Edward, four, were still kept out of the limelight.

MEETING some of the fellows of Somerville College, Oxford, on 2 May (below). The Queen never went to university, and as R.A. Butler, the Master of Trinity College, Cambridge, said, 'Quite frankly, the Queen and the Duke are not university people – they're horsy people, commonsense people. The Queen is one of the most intelligent women in England and brilliant in summing up people, but I don't think she's awfully interested in books. You never see any lying about her room . . . just newspapers and things like that.'

THE FAMILY gather on the balcony at Buckingham Palace (left) for the annual Trooping the Colour in June. From left to right, in the front row: Marina Ogilvy, Prince Andrew, Lord Nicholas Windsor, Lady Helen Windsor, Prince Edward, and Viscount David Linley. In the back row: the Queen Mother, the Duchess of Kent, Princess Alexandra, the Duke of Kent, the Queen, Lord Snowdon, Princess Marina, and Princess Margaret.

IN NOVEMBER the Queen and the Duke of Edinburgh were in South America, where they were greeted with great enthusiasm by the crowds. After ten days in Brazil (right), they spent a further eight days in Chile. The Queen was clearly enjoying herself at a visit to a local school, the Escuela Inglaterra (above), where she was guarded by children on bicycles, dressed up to look like Coldstream Guards. To the Queen's left is the President's wife, Señora Maria Ruiz Tagle de Frei.

NEWS IN BRIEF

1 Jan – 'I'm backing Britain' campaign is launched

5 Jan – Alexander Dubcek, a liberal reformist, is elected leader of the Czechoslovakian Communist Party

31 Jan – The Beatles set up their Apple boutique in London

31 Jan – The Communist Viet Cong of North Vietnam launch the 'Tet offensive', attacks on major cities in South Vietnam

4 Apr – Martin Luther King, the black civil rights leader, is shot dead in Memphis, aged 39

21 Apr – Enoch Powell predicts a 'river of blood' if immigration to Britain is not reduced

23 Apr – The first decimal coins are brought into circulation -- 5 new pence and 10 new pence

16 May – The Ronan Point block of flats 'collapses'

6 Jun – Senator Robert Kennedy is shot dead, aged 42

24 Jun – Comedian Tony Hancock dies

22 Aug – Soviet tanks enter the Czech capital to crush the 'Prague spring'

16 Sep – A two-tier postal system is introduced: first-class letters cost 5d, second-class 4d

18 Oct – Beatle John Lennon and his girlfriend, Yoko Ono, are arrested on drug charges

1 Nov – President Johnson orders a halt to US bombings in Vietnam

6 Nov – Richard Nixon is elected President of the USA

25 Dec – In her Christmas Speech, the Queen makes a plea for racial tolerance

A SMILING sovereign, bedecked with the robes and jewels of the Order of St Michael and St George (left) is helped into her waiting car by a page boy as she leaves St Paul's Cathedral. The decorative Order is of feudal origin, and is most commonly awarded to members of the diplomatic service and others who have undertaken distinguished service abroad. In June, the Queen invested Prince Charles as a Knight of the Order of the Garter.

THE QUEEN delivering a speech at the Centenary Banquet of the Trades Union Congress at the Guildhall on 5 June (left). While the TUC had indisputably improved the working conditions of millions of people in Britain, the years of the Queen's reign had seen a dramatic rise in strikes, which were becoming ever-more disruptive. TUC policy is decided at their annual Conference in September. Representation is based on one delegate per 5,000 members, affording large unions a huge 'block vote'.

1969

Concern for the safety of her eldest son affected the Queen for much of the year as his Investiture as Prince of Wales drew closer. The plan was for Prince Charles to spend eight weeks before the ceremony at the University of Wales in Aberystwyth, where he would learn the language and something of the culture and history of the Principality. Shortly before the start of term, however, George Thomas, Secretary of State for Wales, received a letter from the Principal of the University, expressing grave fears about the current atmosphere in the town and indicating that he could not accept responsibility for the Prince's safety. Everyone knew that if the Prince could not go to Aberystwyth, there would be no Investiture, and part of the United Kingdom would effectively become a no-go area to members of the royal family. The risk had to be taken.

Prince Charles suffered taunts and abuse, and, prepared as he was, he had never met such naked hostility; but he faced his critics and mastered the language sufficiently to address an audience of 5,000 at the Welsh League of Youth Eisteddfod in Welsh. The stage was now set for one of the most spectacular occasions of the Queen's reign and one of the most significant days of Charles's life.

THE QUEEN revelling in a rare trip on the London Underground on 7 March (right), when she opened the new Victoria Line which would eventually run from Brixton in the south, through Victoria and the West End of London, and via King's Cross to Walthamstow in the north-east.

VICTORIA LINE

7 MARCH 1969

PRINCE CHARLES'S Investiture as Prince of Wales on 1 July went ahead without incident, although two bombs exploded during the course of the day, one on the railway line along which the royal train travelled, killing the two men who planted it. The other went off in a field within earshot of the Prince, as he made his way by horse-drawn coach to Caernarvon Castle. It was a day of magnificent and glorious pageantry, a masterpiece of stage-management and design. 'I think my view of the situation', said the Prince, when asked about the cost, 'is that if you are going to have a ceremony like this you should spend enough money to make it dignified, colourful and worthy of Britain.' It might, he said, 'perhaps take people's minds off the economic squeeze for a moment or two.'

Most of the cost went on design, co-ordinated by Lord Snowdon in his role as Constable of Caernarvon. It was a dramatic mixture of ancient and ultra-modern. The soaring stone walls of the castle were emblazoned with tall, white banners with red dragons, all made of expanded polystyrene. Banks of red chairs created a perfect theatre in the round, and at the focal point, beneath a canopy of clear perspex bearing the Prince of Wales feathers stood three thrones of riven Welsh slate

on a circular slate dais, where the Queen and the Duke of Edinburgh took their seats (right). Dressed in the blue uniform of the Royal Regiment of Wales, Charles was brought from the Chamberlain Tower to kneel on a cushion before his mother (above). She then invested him with the ancient symbols: a sword, a coronet, a gold ring, and a gold rod. The Prince paid homage to his sovereign, gave her a kiss of fealty and took his place on the throne to her right. The ceremony has scarcely changed since Edward III invested the Black Prince in 1343.

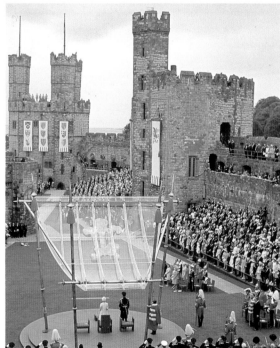

The new decade brought change, and new hope. A General Election on 19 June brought the Conservative Party back into power with a majority of thirty. Edward Heath, who had succeeded Alec Douglas-Home as party leader in 1965, became Prime Minister. Unlike the Queen's previous Tory Prime Ministers, who had all been educated at public school (Churchill at Harrow, the others all at Eton), Heath was of a different mould. He had attended a grammar school in Ramsgate, and had then won a scholarship to Balliol College, Oxford, where he became President of the Oxford Union. After the genial Yorkshire bluntness of Harold Wilson, which the Queen had come to enjoy, Heath was very much a cold fish. A bachelor, his passions were sailing and music, leaving him with little in common with the Queen.

Both of the Queen's elder children had meanwhile begun taking on official duties: Charles had graduated from Cambridge in June, and had taken his seat in the House of Lords; in November he represented the Queen at the funeral of President de Gaulle. And Princess Anne had become President of the Save the Children Fund, a role that would later become her major concern.

1970

THE QUEEN MOTHER looking radiant at seventy, complemented by a blaze of rhododendron flowers (right). The Queen Mother is an enormously enthusiastic gardener; she transformed the gardens at Buckingham Palace during her tenure, and although the enthusiasm has passed her daughters by, Prince Charles has inherited her love of the soil and is a keen organic gardener.

THE QUEEN did not see eye to eye with her new Prime Minister on many subjects, yet it was during Edward Heath's tenancy that the Queen made her first-ever visit to Chequers, the Prime Minister's official country residence in Buckinghamshire. She joined Richard Nixon and his wife, Pat, there (left), when the American President visited Britain in October. The Nixons had played host to Prince Charles and Princess Anne in Washington.

AT THE BEGINNING of March the Queen and the Duke of Edinburgh, accompanied by Princess Anne, left Britain for another tour of the Antipodes, looking in briefly at Fiji and Tonga on the way. They joined the royal yacht *Britannia* in the South Pacific, and, sailing into the Cook Strait between the North and South Islands of New Zealand, encountered a heavy storm, during which three sailors were swept overboard. Prince Philip helped in a dramatic rescue operation, but one of the men was sadly lost.

The royal party spent two weeks in New Zealand, then over a month in Australia, where they sensed a wind of change. It was a country moving towards republicanism, and a Gallup poll showed that fifty-one per cent of Australians no longer wanted 'God Save the Queen' as their National Anthem. But there was no keeping away the more patriotic citizens (above), and the Queen was given a warm welcome by the crowds, some lucky enough to be singled out for a private word with their sovereign (right and opposite below).

THE QUEEN chatting cheerfully to Princess Anne in Fiji (left) during a break in a Maori display in the capital, Suva, in early March. The Queen enjoyed having her daughter with her, and was pleased with the way she was beginning to take to public life. She had been carrying out solo engagements for the past year, and on New Year's Day had become President of the Save the Children Fund; but when she was not working or accompanying her parents on foreign trips, Princess Anne was in serious training as a three-day eventer. She had found a trainer in Alison Oliver, one of the most celebrated instructors in the country. It was hard work: every morning she would be up at the crack of dawn to ride for three hours before her official duties began, returning to her horses – Doublet, Purple Star and Royal Ocean – at the end of the day.

THE DUKE of Edinburgh with Emperor Hirohito of Japan (below) during his controversial visit to Britain with the Empress in early October. The tabloid papers referred to him as a war criminal for the part he played in World War II, and the satirical magazine, *Private Eye*, famous for its irreverent covers, showed a picture of Hirohito's aeroplane landing at Gatwick with the caption, 'There's a nasty nip in the air.'

The Badminton Horse Trials comprise the most difficult cross-country course in Britain and attract the best riders in the world. In April, Princess Anne competed on her horse Doublet, and rode as if her life depended upon it, coming fifth overall. Two weeks later she was selected to ride in the European Championships at Burghley in September. In the midst of her training, however, she collapsed in pain and was rushed into hospital in August for the removal of an ovarian cyst. It looked as though her chances were over; but such was her determination that, just weeks later, she won the three-day event and became European Champion. Anne was riding on a wave of popularity. She was voted Sports Personality of the Year by television viewers, and on 5 November the Press declared her Sportswoman of 1971.

Prince Charles in the meantime, after six months in the RAF flying supersonic jets and jumping out of aeroplanes, which unnerved his mother, transferred to the Navy.

NEWS
IN BRIEF

1 Jan – The new law decrees 'irretrievable breakdown of marriage' acceptable as the sole grounds for divorce

2 Jan – Disaster strikes at Ibrox Park as 66 football fans are crushed to death

10 Jan – Coco Chanel dies in Paris

25 Jan – President Obote of Uganda is overthrown in a military coup led by General Idi Amin

15 Feb – Decimal currency is introduced in Britain

26 Mar – Civil war erupts when East Pakistan declares itself the independent state of Bangladesh

8 May – Arsenal win the FA Cup and League title

15 Jun – Education Secretary, Margaret Thatcher, announces plans to end free school milk

6 Jul – 'Satchmo' Louis Armstrong, the jazz legend, dies

17 Jul – Crash helmets are to become compulsory for motor cyclists

15 Aug – Harvey Smith causes furore for apparently making a 2-finger gesture during a show-jumping competition

20 Aug – Prince Charles gets his wings at RAF Cranwell

1 Sep – Penny and threepence coins cease to be legal tender

31 Oct – An IRA bomb explodes in the Post Office Tower

12 Nov – President Nixon announces the withdrawal of 45,000 troops from Vietnam by next February

15 Nov – Chinese delegates take their seats at the United Nations for the first time

THE QUEEN proudly presenting the winner's trophy to Princess Anne at the end of the European Championships at Burghley in September (left). It was a great achievement by any standard, and a measure of Anne's will to succeed.

IN MID-OCTOBER, the Queen, the Duke of Edinburgh and Princess Anne paid a week-long state visit to Turkey (below). To the left, in sunglasses, is the Queen's personal bodyguard, Commander Michael Trestrail.

THE QUEEN shaking hands with the former Secretary of State for War, John Profumo (left), at the opening of Attlee House, a social-welfare centre in the east end of London, where Profumo had worked since his resignation in 1963. The Queen had always been sympathetic towards John Profumo, and never felt that he had posed any security threat by his affair with Christine Keeler. When he resigned she had sent him a personal letter thanking him for all the work he had done as a minister in her governments and expressing sorrow at the unhappy way in which his career had ended. In 1975 she would award him a CBE for his tireless work with the socially disadvantaged in London.

This was a year both of great personal sadness and personal celebration. At the end of March, the Queen returned from a tour of south-east Asia to the news that her uncle, the Duke of Windsor, was gravely ill with cancer at his home in Paris. The Queen very much wanted to see him, and a state visit to France in May provided her with the opportunity. Accompanied by Prince Philip and Prince Charles, the Queen had afternoon tea with the Duchess before being taken upstairs to see the man whose abdication had so radically changed her life. As the Queen came into the room, the emaciated Duke struggled to stand, but she gently insisted he remain seated. When she left, the Queen knew that she was saying goodbye forever.

MEMBERS OF THE Royal Family assembled at Windsor to celebrate the Queen's silver wedding anniversary. From left to right, standing: Lord Snowdon, the Duke of Kent, Prince Michael of Kent, Prince Philip, Prince Charles, Prince Andrew, Angus Ogilvy, James Ogilvy. Seated: Princess Margaret, the Duchess of Kent with Lord Nicholas Windsor on her lap, Queen Elizabeth the Queen Mother, Queen Elizabeth II, the Earl of St Andrews, Princess Anne, Marina Ogilvy, Princess Alexandra. On the floor: Lady Sarah Armstrong-Jones, Viscount Linley, Prince Edward and Lady Helen Windsor.

THE DUKE OF
Windsor died just eight days after the Queen had visited him. His body was flown to London to lie in state in St George's Chapel at Windsor (below) before being buried at Frogmore. The Duchess, confused and grief-stricken, stayed at Buckingham Palace as the Queen's personal guest (right).

NEWS
IN BRIEF
≈

22 Jan – Britain, along with Ireland, Denmark and Norway, joins the EEC

30 Jan – British paratroopers open fire on protestors in Belfast in what becomes known as 'Bloody Sunday'

27 Apr – Five men's colleges at Oxford University vote to admit women for the first time, starting in 1974

2 May – J. Edgar Hoover, founder and long-time Director of the FBI, dies in Washington

26 May – Thomas Cook, the travel agency, is denationalized

28 May – Edward, Duke of Windsor dies in Paris

17 Jun – Five men are arrested while attempting to bug the Democratic National Committee's offices in Watergate, Washington

11 Aug – The last American ground troops withdraw from Vietnam

28 Aug – Prince William of Gloucester is killed in an air race

5 Sep – Arab gunmen open fire on the Israeli building at the Olympic village in Munich, killing two

21 Sep – Asians expelled from Uganda by President Idi Amin begin arriving in Britain

10 Oct – John Betjemen is appointed Poet Laureate

7 Nov – Richard Nixon is re-elected President of USA

15 Nov – A scheme is announced for kidney donor cards

26 Nov – The Race Relations Act becomes law, making it illegal to discrimate on grounds of colour

26 Dec – Harry S. Truman, 33rd President of the USA, dies

EARLY IN FEBRUARY, accompanied by the Duke of Edinburgh and Princess Anne, the Queen enjoyed a colourful – if hot – state visit to Thailand (above). From there they travelled to Indonesia, Singapore, Malaysia, Brunei, the Maldives and the Seychelles, before flying home at the end of March via Mauritius and Kenya. They covered a total of 24,000 miles, and much of it in intense heat. In Malacca (right), they were joined by Earl Mountbatten, who, since his retirement, travelled the world as a roving ambassador, sometimes alone, sometimes escorting members of the royal family, and almost always seizing the opportunity to proselytize and raise money for his favourite organization, the United World Colleges. These were a growing number of international schools aiming to promote peace through racial understanding.

THE QUEEN clearly enjoying the company of President Tito and his wife during a four-day visit to Yugoslavia in October (right), her first-ever visit to a Communist country. Accompanied by the Duke of Edinburgh and Princess Anne, she arrived to a rapturous welcome, and thoroughly enjoyed her stay. In four days they were treated to some breathtaking scenery as they were driven through the mountains. They also planted a peace tree in Friendship Park near the River Danube, and did some sight-seeing in Dubrovnik.

CAPTAIN MARK PHILLIPS, a fellow competitor at the Burghley Horse Trials in September, talking to Princess Anne as she awaits her turn for the dressage competition (below). They had been riding in the same events up and down the country for the past three years and had become close friends.

PRINCE WILLIAM of Gloucester leaving the church after the wedding of his younger brother, Richard, to Brigitte van Deurs (left). Also in the picture are his mother, the Duchess of Gloucester on the left and Princess Alice, Countess of Athlone. Just a few weeks later, on 28 August, the thirty-year-old Prince, much loved by the whole royal family, was killed in an air race, when his light aircraft crashed shortly after take-off.

1972

ALTHOUGH protocol insists that the Duke of Edinburgh takes second place to his wife in public life, in private and in family matters, their roles are very traditional: it is he who makes the decisions, and Elizabeth is happy to defer to her husband. Her family are vitally important to the Queen and she relishes time spent with them, which is why she so jealously guards her traditional holiday periods. These are the times when she is able to enjoy her children to the full, particularly the long break at the end of the summer when they congregate in the Highlands – often with extended family too. Here they can lower their guard, relax among trusted friends and retainers, and simply be themselves. The Queen goes for long walks with her dogs (above) and when the weather is up to it, the family give the chefs a rest and barbecue. Prince Philip and Princess Anne are in charge of the meat (right).

1972

*O*n a particularly joyful personal note, 20 November marked the Queen and the Duke of Edinburgh's silver-wedding anniversary, which was celebrated by a special service in Westminster Abbey and a large family get-together at Windsor Castle. In a touching speech at the Guildhall, where the Queen had luncheon after the service, she said, 'When the Bishop was asked what he thought about sin, he replied with simple conviction that he was against it. If I am asked today what I think about family life after twenty-five years of marriage, I can answer with equal simplicity and conviction. I am for it.'

THE QUEEN riding through the heather on the Balmoral Estate (below). The house itself, which has been in the family since its purchase by Queen Victoria in 1852, is in the background. Unlike Buckingham Palace and Windsor Castle, which belong to the state, Balmoral – like Sandringham – is privately owned by the Queen; and there are few places where she is happier.

1973

The optimism with which the year began, with Britain's entry at long last into the European Economic Community, was short-lived: 1973 turned into a year of industrial unrest and strikes, including a miners' overtime ban which so crippled the country that by December, in order to conserve energy, a three-day working week was announced. Electricity users were only allowed sixty-five per cent of their normal consumption, and a fifty m.p.h. speed limit was imposed on the roads to save fuel.

The news, on 29 May, that Princess Anne was to marry Lieutenant Mark Phillips in November was a welcome distraction from the gloom and despondency. It was so obviously a love match. Mark was no aristocrat; but, in common with Anne, he loved horses, and at the age of twenty-five he was already a first-class equestrian. He had been to Mexico with the British Olympic Team in 1968, and he had twice won at Badminton.

BADMINTON Horse Trials in April, and a typical picture of the Queen off-duty with her family: wrapped in a warm winter coat, woolly stockings and the ubiquitous headscarf, with a camera to her eye (below). Also in the picture are Princess Margaret, the Queen Mother, Prince Edward, looking intently through binoculars in the other direction, and Sarah Armstrong-Jones.

NEWS
IN BRIEF

11 Jan – The Open University awards its first degrees to students

23 Jan – President Nixon announces a ceasefire in Vietnam

1 Feb – The Stock Exchange floor in London is open to women for the first time

8 Feb – A new inquiry is ordered into the Watergate burglary

26 Mar – Noel Coward, master of English wit, dies, aged 73

31 Mar – Red Rum wins the Grand National in a record time

1 Apr – VAT is introduced in the new Budget

8 Apr – Pablo Picasso, the most famous painter of the century, dies, aged 91

29 Apr – President Nixon denies any personal involvement in the Watergate affair

29 May – Buckingham Palace announces the engagement of Princess Anne to Lieutenant Mark Phillips

28 Aug – Princess Anne visits Russia, the first member of the royal family to do so

15 Sep – Japanese car-firm, Datsun, accounts for 1 in 20 new cars sold in Britain

6 Oct – Egypt and Syria attack Israel during Yom Kippur, the holiest day in the Jewish calender

17 Oct – The oil crisis escalates as Arab states announce massive increase in price of oil

17 Dec – An emergency budget massively cuts public spending, limits electricity consumption and puts Britain on a three-day working week

THE DUKE of Edinburgh arriving in Moscow in September (left) for the three-day European Horse Trials in Kiev, in his capacity as President of the International Equestrian Federation. Princess Anne (opposite below right) was competing. On the second day of the event she had a bad fall over a jump that had been the undoing of over thirty other horses. She landed heavily, chipping her shoulder blade and dislocating her collar bone in the process. Jeopardizing her relationship with the Press photographers, she snapped, 'I hope you've got your money's worth now.'

THE QUEEN officially opening the famous Sydney Opera House in Australia on 20 October before a crowd of 15,000 guests (below). The complex was designed by the Danish architect, Joern Utzon, who won an international competition for its design in 1956. The eventual cost rose from an original estimate of A $7.5 million, to a staggering A $102 million, and much of the money was raised by a New South Wales Government lottery.

ANNE AND MARK were married on 14 November, coincidentally Prince Charles's twenty-fifth birthday. Anne had hoped to have a quiet, private wedding, but the Queen was not to be done out of giving her only daughter a proper send-off. Schoolchildren had a day's holiday, and people turned out in their thousands to watch the Princess make the journey by glass coach to Westminster Abbey. Prince Edward and Lady Sarah Armstrong-Jones, both aged nine, attended the bride. The ceremony was televised (right), but the Princess refused to allow the cameras to capture the moment when Mark placed the ring on her finger. After the usual appearance on the balcony, and the official photograph (right) the newly-weds spent the night at Princess Alexandra's home, Thatched House Lodge, in Richmond, before flying to Barbados the next day to join *Britannia* for a honeymoon at sea. They then paid official visits to Antigua, Colombia, Equador (above), Jamaica and Monserrat, using the royal yacht as a base as it made its way south to coincide with the Queen's arrival in New Zealand at the end of January the following year.

1974
1952~1992~1992~1952~1992~1952

The Queen was in Indonesia when she learned that Princess Anne had narrowly escaped death in a dramatic and frightening kidnap attempt in London, which left four men wounded, one seriously. She and Mark Phillips were being driven down the Mall, on their way back from an early evening engagement, when, within a few hundred yards of Buckingham Palace, a car suddenly swerved in front of their car forcing it to stop. A gunman leapt out and fired a shot into the car, then ran around to the Princess's door and tried to drag her out, ripping her sleeve in the process. Also in the car was her bodyguard, Inspector James Beaton, and a lady-in-waiting. In the frenzy that followed, Beaton, the chauffeur, a policeman who came to assist, and the driver of the car behind were all shot.

The shock waves were felt far and wide and Harold Wilson, as Prime Minister, ordered an urgent enquiry into the incident. The entire security of the royal family was given a thorough review, and from that day forth their cars have been bullet-proofed, and the route taken on annual journeys, such as to the Cenotaph on Remembrance Sunday, is often varied.

PRINCESS ANNE visiting her bodyguard, Inspector James Beaton, at Westminster Hospital (below), where he was taken with bullet wounds after thwarting an attempt to kidnap the Princess on 20 March. She also visited the three others who were injured in the attack. Earl Mountbatten was with the Queen and Prince Philip in Indonesia when news of the incident reached them. He congratulated the Prince on the courage Anne had shown. 'If the man had succeeded in abducting Anne,' said her father proudly, 'she would have given him a hell of a time while in captivity.'

THE QUEEN sharing a joke (right) with one of her bodyguards as she sits amongst the Yeoman of the Guard in the grounds of Buckingham Palace.

THE QUEEN with the Duke of Edinburgh (below) during the ceremony of the Most Noble Order of the Garter. The Order was founded in 1348 by King Edward III and is the highest ranking Order in Great Britain, originally limited to the sovereign and twenty-five knights. That number has been extended, but it is still not a common honour. The Garter is worn below the left knee by men, and as a sash draped over the left shoulder by women.

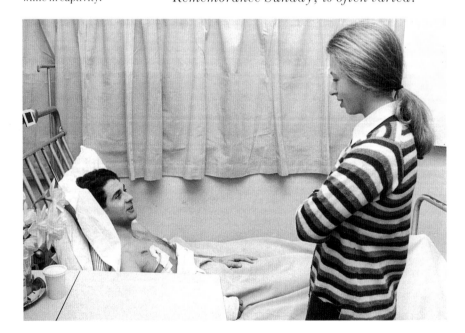

NEWS IN BRIEF

~

6 Mar – Harold Wilson becomes Prime Minister

15 Mar – President Nixon is found guilty by a federal grand jury of conspiracy to cover up the Watergate burglary

3 Apr – Glenda Jackson wins an Oscar for *A Touch of Class*

15 Apr – Heiress Patty Hearst, kidnapped by the Symbionese Liberation Army, takes part in a bank robbery in San Francisco

1 May – Alf Ramsay is sacked as England soccer manager

18 May – India becomes the sixth nation to develop an atomic bomb

19 May – Valerie Giscard d'Estaing is elected President of France

13 Jun – Prince Charles makes his maiden speech in the House of Lords

Jul 6 – Jimmy Connors wins the men's singles title at Wimbledon; his fiancée, Chris Evert, is the ladies' champion

8 Aug – Richard Nixon resigns as US President; he is succeeded by Gerald Ford

14 Sep – Two giant pandas, gifts of the Chinese government, arrive at London Zoo

1 Oct – Macdonald's first hamburger restaurant in Britain opens in south London

11 Oct – The General Election re-elects Wilson's government with an overall majority of just three seats

12 Nov – Lord Lucan is sought for the murder of his children's nanny

21 Nov – IRA bombs in two Birmingham pubs explode, killing 17

THE QUEEN at Buckingham Palace with Sir Dawda Jawara, President of The Gambia, as they make their way to the forecourt to inspect the 1st Battalion of Welsh Guards (left). Despite the colourful robes, Dawda Jawara, whose country broke away from the Commonwealth and became a republic in 1970, is no stranger to Britain nor to the western way of life. He was a student at Glasgow University where he qualified as a veterinary surgeon in the 1950s.

THE QUEEN, travelling with the Duke of Edinburgh, Princess Anne and her new husband, Mark Phillips, meet the famous 'Mudmen' in Papua, New Guinea (above left), the island's traditional warriors. More tradition, Polynesian style (left) in Raratonga, the largest of the Cook Islands, where the party made a flying visit in February. They were met by the Prime Minister, Sir Albert Royal Henry, and his wife.

AT THE END of April the Danish royals, Queen Margrethe and Prince Henrik, paid a state visit to Britain. After arriving in Greenwich, South London, they travelled to Windsor Castle (above) where they stayed as guests of the Queen and Prince Philip.

A RARE SIGHT of the Queen wearing trousers (far left) – evidently well chosen given the terrain – for an expedition off the beaten track in New Zealand.

The discovery of oil in the North Sea was a tremendous boost to the British economy. It began flowing in June, brought ashore to the refinery by tanker, and in November the Queen formally inaugurated the first underwater pipeline. But the advent of North Sea oil added fuel to the growing demand for Home Rule by the Scottish Nationalists, which had been gaining momentum over the years, as they bitterly resented the profits from their oil going straight to London. The SNP elected its first member to Westminster in 1970, and in the latest election in October 1974, the party had won eleven seats in the House of Commons. Welsh nationalism was on the increase too. The Queen raised the issue for the first time in her speech at the Opening of Parliament in November, promising far more autonomy for Scotland and Wales.

The Queen was abroad again for much of the early part of the year, visiting the Bahamas, Mexico, Hong Kong and Japan. In November Prince Philip went to Madrid for the Coronation of Prince Juan Carlos, while back in Britain the Queen installed Prince Charles as Great Master of the Order of Bath.

A DELIGHTED owner congratulating her horse and jockey after a successful race at Ascot (below). The Duke of Edinburgh stalking in the background is an unenthusiastic visitor to the racecourse, but does his duty at Royal Ascot in June. It is a high spot in the social calendar, and has had royal patronage since horse-races were first run on Ascot Heath during the reign of Queen Anne in 1711. The event is a special favourite with the Queen, particularly when her own horses are amongst the winners.

A FAMILY GATHERING of British, Greek, Dutch and Danish royals on 8 March (right) for the wedding of Patrick, Earl of Lichfield, to Lady Leonora Grosvenor, daughter of the Duke of Westminster.

THE QUEEN with Prince Charles (below), about to be installed as Great Master of the Order of Bath. He was greatly amused having had no bath for the past month while living under canvas in the Arctic. He had grown a beard, but shaved it off for the ceremony. The next day the moustache was gone.

NEWS IN BRIEF

4 Feb – Margaret Thatcher defeats Edward Heath in the first ballot for the leadership of the Conservative Party; she becomes leader after a second ballot on 11 Feb

19 Feb – The Queen, on her tour of Barbados, knights cricket star, Gary Sobers

28 Feb – A crash at Moorgate tube station kills 35

17 Apr – Cambodia falls to the Khmer Rouge, Communist forces commanded by Pol Pot

24 Apr – Unemployment in Britain passes the one million mark

31 Apr – Saigon, the capital of South Vietnam, surrenders to Communist North Vietnam; America organizes a mass evacuation of personnel; the war is over

9 Jun – Debates in the House of Commons are broadcast live on radio for the first time

11 Jul – Chinese archaeologists announce the discovery of a 'terracotta army' near Xi'an

11 Jul – The Prosecution at the trial of the 'Birmingham Six' admits the accused were seriously assaulted whilst in police custody

28 Oct – Armed robbers hold 7 Italians hostage in a siege of the Spaghetti House restaurant in Knightsbridge, London

20 Nov – General Franco, Spain's military dictator, dies, aged 82

25 Nov – King Juan Carlos, Spain's new leader, declares an amnesty to mark his accession

6 Dec – Four IRA gunmen take a married couple hostage in their flat in Balcombe Street, London

THE QUEEN enjoying herself at a market stall during her visit to Hong Kong in early May (left). However tempting and exotic the produce, she was definitely just looking. Despite the handbag that goes everywhere with her, the Queen never carries money in it. On the very rare occasions when she might wish to buy something, an equerry will always pay. On her travels around the world, Elizabeth has been honoured with some weird and wonderful local delicacies, but she has a golden rule that she will never eat oysters, lobsters and other shellfish. This is simply a safety precaution, for the same reason the Queen never drinks local water, but takes still mineral water wherever she goes.

IN CHINESE culture, dragons are often benevolent, although they need to be courted with gifts. Here, the Queen is seen painting in the eyes on a dragon mask in Hong Kong, prior to the performance of a dragon dance (left). Dragon dances are most commonly performed during celebrations of the Chinese New Year, where the beasts represent the gifts of fertility and renewal.

THE QUEEN with Emperor Hirohito (left) arriving at a state banquet during the Queen and the Duke of Edinburgh's five-day state visit to Japan in May. The Queen and Emperor Hirohito share a toast (below). Standing between them is an interpreter and court official of the Imperial Household, Hideki Mazaki. It was a significant visit, the first by a member of the royal family since the War, and a diplomatic mending of bridges, following on from the Emperor's visit to London in 1969. The return visit had taken nearly six years to organize, and involved extensive talks between Buckingham Palace, the Foreign Office, the British Embassy and the Japanese Foreign Ministry.

In March Harold Wilson suddenly resigned. He was in ill health and intended to retire from politics. Wilson and the Queen had had a good working relationship, and had enjoyed their weekly meetings, as the Queen's visit to Downing Street with Prince Philip for a farewell dinner bore witness. It was the first time she had been there since dining with Churchill on his retirement in 1955. Wilson in turn paid tribute to his sovereign in his retirement speech: 'I shall certainly advise my successor', who was to be James Callaghan, 'to do his homework before his audience, and to read all his telegrams and Cabinet Committee papers in time, and not leave them to the weekend, or he will feel like an unprepared schoolboy.'

In April the Queen celebrated her fiftieth birthday, surrounded as ever by her family, but there was considerable sadness amongst them over the breakdown of Princess Margaret's marriage. They were all deeply fond of Lord Snowdon, but the marriage had been under considerable strain from the start. The transition from commoner to royal appendage had been difficult and somewhat emasculating; and Margaret was no easy woman to live with.

THE QUEEN MOTHER (right) with Princess Margaret and Lady Sarah Armstrong-Jones watching the action at Badminton in April, comfortably settled on the ground; and at the end of the day, as they pack up to go home (far right), the Queen holds one of her dogs at arms' length to keep its muddy paws away, as she waits for her niece to get into the car first.

1976

PRINCE PHILIP competing in the four-in-hand Grand Prix at Windsor (right). His first love had always been polo, to which he had introduced his eldest son, but worsening arthritis in his hand eventually forced him to give up polo for the less exacting sport of four-in-hand. Although less physical, it is not without its dangers. The Queen and the Duke of Edinburgh once stopped a team of runaway horses. The Queen ran into their path and waved her arms in the air, while the Duke tried to catch hold of one of the horses' bridles.

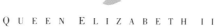

THE QUEEN and her diminished family (left) pose for her fiftieth-birthday portrait in April. Prince Edward was the only one of the children still living close enough to home to be present for the photograph, but even he was at boarding-school, at Heatherdown in Ascot. Prince Charles was at sea, in the minehunter, HMS *Bronington*, over which he had command from February until he left the Navy in December. Princess Anne was living in a rented house at Sandhurst, where Mark Phillips, now a Captain, was an instructor; and Prince Andrew was at Gordonstoun, enjoying his time there far more than his elder brother ever had.

NEWS
IN BRIEF
〜

12 Jan – Agatha Christie, 'Queen' of crime writers, dies, aged 85

21 Jan – The Concorde supersonic aeroplane makes its first commercial flight

18 Feb – The Tate Gallery's acquisition of a pile of bricks by Carl Andre causes controversy

1 Mar – MPs approve a Bill to make the wearing of seat belts in cars compulsory

24 Mar – Field Marshal Bernard Montgomery dies, aged 80

5 Apr – James Callaghan is appointed Prime Minister

5 Apr – Howard Hughes, multi-millionaire recluse, dies, aged 70

27 Jun – Palestinians hijack an Air France plane; the plane eventually lands at Entebbe Airport, Uganda

3 Jul – Bjorn Borg wins the men's singles final at Wimbledon, the first Swede ever, and the youngest champion for 45 years

4 Jul – Israeli troops storm the 'skyjacked' plane at Entebbe

7 Jul – David Steel is elected new leader of the Liberal Party, replacing Jeremy Thorpe

17 Jul – The Queen opens the Olympic Games in Montreal

31 Aug – Fierce race riots mar the Notting Hill carnival in west London

9 Sep – Chairman Mao Tse-tung of China dies, aged 82

26 Oct – The Queen opens the National Theatre

2 Nov – Jimmy Carter is elected President of the USA

4 Dec – Benjamin Britten, composer, dies, aged 63

IN JULY the Queen and the Duke of Edinburgh flew to America on a five-day state visit for the bicentennial celebrations. It was the first time the Queen had been to the United States in nineteen years, and the first time she had met the new President, Gerald Ford. With the statue of George Washington, the man responsible, towering above her (left), his left leg just visible, the Queen added her voice to the country's delight at 200 years of freedom from British rule. It was an enjoyable and relaxed visit, and the Queen was clearly in high spirits (below) with Gerald Ford and his wife at a reception and banquet he held in her honour at the White House. Amongst other celebrities she met the boxing legend, Mohammed Ali, and one of her favourite actors, *Kojak* star, Telly Savalas.

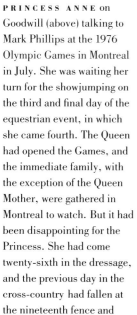

PRINCESS ANNE on Goodwill (above) talking to Mark Phillips at the 1976 Olympic Games in Montreal in July. She was waiting her turn for the showjumping on the third and final day of the equestrian event, in which she came fourth. The Queen had opened the Games, and the immediate family, with the exception of the Queen Mother, were gathered in Montreal to watch. But it had been disappointing for the Princess. She had come twenty-sixth in the dressage, and the previous day in the cross-country had fallen at the nineteenth fence and

suffered severe concussion. But such was her determination that, to everyone's astonishment, she climbed back on her horse and completed the course. Anne had always dreamt of making the British Olympic Team, and had been selected after winning a silver medal in the European Championships in West Germany the previous year, but she came away from Montreal feeling depressed. Mark Phillips had been in the reserve team, but in the event, did not have a chance to compete.

THE QUEEN standing next to one of the famous Canadian Mounties (above).

IN NOVEMBER, the Queen and the Duke paid a state visit to Luxemburg (left), followed by a couple of days spent privately with the Grand Duke Jean, an old family friend. It was his daughter, Princess Marie Astrid, a Roman Catholic, who was later said by the Press to be going to marry Prince Charles. In reality, they had scarcely met.

1977

The year was largely dominated by the Queen's Silver Jubilee celebrations. Preparations had been under way for some time for the most extensive tour the monarch had ever undertaken of both the United Kingdom and the Commonwealth. If Elizabeth was ever in doubt about her popularity, 1977 put an end to it. There was public euphoria. Everywhere she went she was touched and delighted by the warmth and enthusiasm of her reception. She seemed more relaxed than ever as she mingled with the crowds that turned out in their thousands to greet her.

In June, more than a million people packed on to the streets of London for a thanksgiving service in St Paul's Cathedral, even more than had turned out for the Coronation. In a repetition of that day, the Queen once again travelled from Buckingham Palace in the gold state coach pulled by eight Windsor greys, flanked by grooms in scarlet and gold uniform, and all the pomp and majesty that a royal occasion could muster. Prince Philip sat in the coach alongside his wife, and Prince Charles rode close behind.

CROWDS CHEER and wave to the Queen and Prince Philip on a visit to Ulster in March (right), apparently unmoved by the serious threats of violence from the IRA. The Queen has never allowed terrorism or the menace of personal danger to deter her from her intended programme. She has come to accept that bodyguards and security precautions are essential, although having lived much of her life without heavy security, she doesn't much care for it. She has always been determined, however, that to allow fear to rule her life would be to concede a victory to terrorism.

NEWS
IN BRIEF

17 Jan – Gary Gilmore is the first prisoner in over 10 years to be executed in the USA

2 Feb – Paris's ultra-modern Pompidou Centre is opened

27 Mar – Two jumbo jets collide on take-off from the Canary Islands, killing 574 people

24 Mar – The 'Lib-Lab Pact' is formed to preserve Mr Callaghan's Government's majority

2 Apr – Red Rum is the first horse ever to win the Grand National for a third time

6 Jun – Beacons are lit across Britain to mark the beginning of a week of celebrations for the Queen's Silver Jubilee

15 Jun – Spain holds its first democratic elections for 41 years

1 Jul – Virginia Wade wins the women's singles final in Wimbledon's centenary year

5 Jul – Zulfikar Ali Bhutto, Prime Minister of Pakistan, is overthrown by General Zia ul-Haq

11 Aug – Yorkshire cricketer, Geoff Boycott, scores the 100th century of his career

16 Aug – Elvis Presley, the 'King', dies, aged 42

12 Sep – South African black rights leader, Steve Biko, dies whilst in police detention

26 Sep – Freddie Laker's 'walk-on' transatlantic air service, Skytrain, makes its inaugural flight

18 Nov – Egyptian President, Anwar Sadat, flies to Jerusalem for historic peace talks with Israeli Prime Minister, Menachem Begin

25 Dec – Charlie Chaplin, comic genius, dies, aged 88

PRINCE PHILIP with the Queen at the State Opening of Parliament (left). A series of by-election losses had lost the Government its overall majority, and as a result it had entered into an agreement with the Liberal Party in March, which enabled it to fight off a vote of no confidence by the Conservatives. The pact was renewed for the new session of Parliament.

THE QUEEN about to set light to a thirty-foot bonfire on the top of Snow Hill, near Windsor Castle (below), the first of a hundred beacons that illuminated the skies from high ground all over the British Isles, marking the start of the Jubilee celebrations in June.

THE QUEEN leaving Buckingham Palace on 6 June (left) for the thanksgiving service at St Paul's Cathedral in the magnificent 216-year-old golden state coach, which had not been used since her Coronation. She was greeted by an eight-trumpet fanfare; addressing a congregation of nearly three thousand people, the Archbishop of Canterbury, the Most Reverend Donald Coggan, spoke of the Queen's 'service untiringly done'. The Queen then made her way on foot to the Guildhall, in one of the most relaxed encounters ever made with her subjects. She stopped to shake hands and accept bouquets, smiling and talking to the crowds that jostled one another for a closer view of their sovereign.

THE STREETS of London were alive with people, many of them waving Union Jacks, and some even draped in their national flag (left). It was a day of patriotic fervour throughout the land. In cities, towns and villages, there were jubilant street parties, such as this one (above) in Nut Street, Manchester. Not even the sudden downpour could dampen spirits. Young and old mixed and mingled and seemed as excited and enthusiastic as each other. An unlikely looking group of teenagers held a banner which seemed to say it all – 'Liz Rules, OK.'

IN FEBRUARY the Queen and the Duke of Edinburgh began the first stage of the most extensive travelling a British sovereign has ever undertaken in the course of a year. On their arrival in Tonga (above) the Queen was met by the twenty-eight-stone King Taufa'ahau Tuou IV of Tonga, who produced the most colossal and sumptuous feast at the royal palace for his guests. The next stop was Fiji (right), where the Queen was presented with a bouquet by a child dressed in traditional costume, on a local variation

to the red carpet that awaits the Queen in most places she visits. It was the first time she had visited Fiji – apart from an overnight stop four years earlier – since the islands, over 800 in all, gained independence from Britain in 1970. From Fiji she and the Duke travelled on to New Zealand where they stayed for almost two weeks, where crowds turned out in their thousands to greet her (above).

BY EARLY MARCH the Queen was in Australia where she travelled extensively, making a number of walkabouts (above, in Queensland). In Sydney there was an uneasy moment when someone in the crowd threw a placard at the Queen, which narrowly missed her face, but it was the only incident in an otherwise relaxed and enjoyable trip.

WEARING SPECTACLES for the first time in public (right) the Queen reads out her speech at the official opening of the Canadian Parliament in Ottawa in October. The whole month was taken up with foreign travel, to the Bahamas, the British Virgin Islands, Antigua and Barbados. In between tours abroad, the Queen had covered much of Britain, and reviewed 3,000 British troops at Sennelager, West Germany.

THE QUEEN watching Prince Charles playing polo at Smith's Lawn in Windsor Great Park (right). It was a rare moment of relaxation in what was a thoroughly exhausting year. During the course of 1977, in her determination to show herself to as many of her subjects as possible during Jubilee Year, she travelled a total of 7,100 miles in the United Kingdom alone. Of these, 1,600 were covered in the royal train, 1,400 were spent on board *Britannia*, 2,400 were travelled in one of four Rolls-Royces, and the remaining 1,700 miles were covered by air, in one of the three Andovers and two Wessex helicopters of the Queen's flight. Overseas visits accounted for a further 37,000 miles. She took part in 800 events organized in her honour. At times the Queen was shaking up to 5,000 hands a day, and she got through scores of gloves in the process.

Bringing a good year to a perfect end, to her great excitement the Queen became a grandmother on 15 November, when Princess Anne gave birth to a son. Peter Phillips was born in the private Lindo Wing of St Mary's Hospital, Paddington, with the Queen's gynaecologist, Mr George Pinker, in attendance. Mark was also present at the birth, and it was a very proud grandmother who went to visit that very evening, smiling and waving to the crowds that waited patiently outside. Anne and Mark had both made it clear that they wanted no title conferred on Mark when they married, and wanted no titles for their children. The Queen's first grandchild, who became fifth in line to the throne, was therefore the first royal baby in more than five centuries to be born a commoner.

A FAMILY DAY out at Badminton in April: not to be missed, Jubilee or no Jubilee (left). In the picture are Lady Sarah Armstrong-Jones, talking to one of the Duke of Beaufort's hounds, with her mother, Princess Margaret, behind her; and the Queen and Prince Edward. The year was not only a personal triumph for the Queen, her Silver Jubilee Appeal, set up to raise money to enable young people to help others, raised sixteen million pounds in the course of the year. It was run by Prince Charles, who had left the Navy to do so.

PRINCESS ANNE with her son, at Buckingham Palace after his christening (above). In a break with tradition, instead of a royal name he was called Peter, after his paternal grandfather. Also in the picture, clockwise, are Princess Alice, Countess of Athlone, Earl Mountbatten, the Queen and the Queen Mother. By this time Princess Anne and Mark Phillips were living at Gatcombe Park, a 560-acre farm in Gloucestershire.

1978

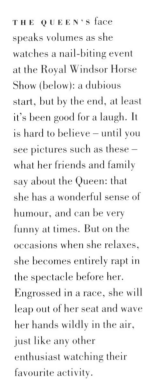

THE QUEEN'S face speaks volumes as she watches a nail-biting event at the Royal Windsor Horse Show (below): a dubious start, but by the end, at least it's been good for a laugh. It is hard to believe – until you see pictures such as these – what her friends and family say about the Queen: that she has a wonderful sense of humour, and can be very funny at times. But on the occasions when she relaxes, she becomes entirely rapt in the spectacle before her. Engrossed in a race, she will leap out of her seat and wave her hands wildly in the air, just like any other enthusiast watching their favourite activity.

*B*ritain was beginning to boom. After years of economic hardship, the tide began to turn, helped by North Sea oil, which was now being exported. Industrial output rose, salaries increased, taxes were reduced, and people had more spending power and general optimism than they had had for decades.

In May Princess Margaret, seriously ill with hepatitis, announced from her hospital bed that she and Lord Snowdon were divorcing. Not long after the decree absolute, Snowdon married Lucy Lindsay-Hogg, former wife of the film and theatre director, Michael Lindsay-Hogg.

Prince Michael of Kent, meanwhile, had plans to marry not only a divorcee, but a Roman Catholic divorcee, Baroness Marie-Christine von Reibnitz, the former Mrs Tom Trowbridge. Although her previous marriage had been annulled, the Pope would not grant permission for her to be married in a Catholic church, and so it fell to the Queen to give permission for the June wedding.

In July the Queen and Prince Philip left for a tour of Canada accompanied by their two younger sons. Andrew, now eighteen, had decided on a naval career like his father, while Edward, at fourteen, was in his second year at Gordonstoun.

13 Feb – Anna Ford joins ITN as their first woman newscaster

25 Feb – Princess Margaret leaves for a holiday in Mustique with Roddy Llewellyn

24 Mar – The *Amoco Cadiz* oiltanker splits in two off the coast of Brittany

30 Mar – The Conservative Party appoints Saatchi & Saatchi to handle their advertising

20 Jun – Joyce McKinney is found guilty, in her absence, of kidnapping a Mormon missionary

26 Jul – Louise Brown, the world's first 'test-tube baby', is born in Manchester

31 Aug – Prince Charles attends the funeral of Jomo Kenyatta, Kenya's leader since independence in 1963

15 Sep – Georgi Markov, a Bulgarian defector, dies after being jabbed by the poisoned tip of an umbrella on Waterloo Bridge, London

18 Sep – President Carter hosts Israeli-Egyptian peace talks at Camp David

30 Sep – Pope John Paul I dies after just 33 days in office

16 Oct – Cardinal Wojtyla of Poland is elected Pope, the first non-Italian since 1542

29 Nov – Members of the People's Temple, a religious cult led by the Rev. Jim Jones, commit mass 'revolutionary suicide' in Jonestown, Guyana; 913 of them die after drinking a potion laced with cyanide

10 Dec – Millions of demonstrators in Teheran call for the Shah to abdicate

CASUALLY DRESSED, the Queen and her mother with Sir John Miller at Badminton in April (above).

THE QUEEN chatting to the Duke of Beaufort at the Royal Windsor Horse Show (above left), one of the most prestigious events in the horsy year. It is held in the Home Park below the Castle, an area not normally open to the public. Competitors and spectators come from all over the world to attend. It is held over a five-day period in May, from Wednesday to Sunday, and as well as civilian events, including the Duke of Edinburgh's four-in-hand driving, which the Queen is inspecting (left), it also features mounted military competitions.

The year began with an exciting three-week tour of the Gulf, visiting Kuwait, Bahrain, Saudi Arabia, Qatar, the United Arab Emirates and Oman. It was the first time the Queen and Prince Philip had visited these oil-rich desert kingdoms, and from a political and commercial point of view, it was a trip of great importance. The Queen had never experienced anything like it. Tactfully dressed in clothes that covered her arms and legs, she was entertained extravagantly, and showered with extraordinary and priceless gifts at every stop. There were banquets in the desert in vast tents hung with silk; they were given exotic spiced food and watched wild dancing. Her hosts even organized a horse-race run on sand dunes for their honoured guest. The Queen enjoyed herself immensely, and at the same time proved invaluable in cementing a firm friendship between Britain and the Arab states.

THE QUEEN with Margaret Thatcher at the Commonwealth Conference in Lusaka, Zambia in July (below). She had returned from the Gulf to find a General Election called for 3 May. The Conservatives returned to power, under the leadership of Margaret Thatcher. For the first time in history, Britain had a woman Prime Minister.

THE QUEEN, perched on a rather unusual seating arrangement (left), listens intently to her host, the Emir of Bahrain, at a horse-race in the baking-hot desert.

DIPLOMATICALLY dressed, the Queen arrives in Saudi Arabia on Concorde on 17 February (below). To overcome the problem of greeting a woman in the land of purdah, the Queen was designated an 'honorary gentleman'. In Qatar, she took tea with the Emir's senior wife, Sheikha Roda, who explained how the Emir's four wives rotated.

THE QUEEN reviewing troops (below left) during a state visit to Tanzania in mid-July.

1979

On 27 August came the shocking news that Lord Mountbatten had been murdered. He had been spending the month with his family at their holiday home in County Sligo in the Republic of Ireland. A fifty-pound bomb exploded as he set out from the little harbour of Mullaghmore to inspect lobster pots. Mountbatten died instantly. Also in the boat were his daughter, Patricia, and her husband, John (Lord and Lady Brabourne), their fourteen-year-old twin sons, Nicholas and Timothy, Lord Brabourne's elderly mother, Doreen, and a local boy named Paul Maxwell. Nicholas and Paul died instantly also. Lady Brabourne senior died the next day. The remainder survived with crippling injuries.

PRINCE CHARLES with Earl Mountbatten, the man he called 'Honorary Grandfather' (below). Theirs was a very special relationship, particularly since Mountbatten's retirement, when he had taken the young Prince under his wing. He was both friend and mentor.

DRESSED IN FULL naval ceremonial uniform, father and son (above left) follow Mountbatten's coffin on its sad journey to Westminster Abbey on 5 September where, in deep mourning, the Queen waits (above). Fighting back tears, Prince Charles read the lesson chosen by Mountbatten before his death (left). It was Psalm 107, 'They that go down to the sea in ships . . .' In claiming responsibility for the 'execution' the IRA said, 'We will tear out their sentimental, imperialist heart.' But the assassination only served to harden the resolve of the 'ruling class' against all manifestations of terrorism.

1952~1992
1952~1992
1980

*S*peculation over whom the Prince of Wales would marry had become an obsession of the tabloid Press, which the entire family found extremely irritating – and none more so than the beleaguered Prince. He would be thirty-two in November, and he could scarcely shake hands with a girl without stories appearing that this was the future Princess of Wales, which made finding a suitable bride extremely difficult. Most girls were frightened off, and the likelihood of the Prince getting to know anyone quietly, without her vital statistics, ancestry, and past history being front-page news, was almost impossible.

During the summer of 1980, however, he fell in love with Lady Diana Spencer, the nineteen-year-old sister of an ex-girlfriend. Diana was the daughter of an Earl, who had been an equerry to the Queen and to George VI before her. Her pedigree was impeccable.

A MOTHER and her two daughters (below): a study by royal photographer, Norman Parkinson, taken to mark the Queen Mother's eightieth birthday on 4 August. There could have been no better birthday present for the Queen Mother than the knowledge that her eldest grandson was falling in love with someone whom she thought would make a perfect wife for him.

LADY DIANA SPENCER (left) with two children from the New England Kindergarten, where she worked, poses obligingly for photographers, unaware that the sunlight has made her skirt see-through. Because she was so young no one had paid any attention when she had been seen with the Prince. Even Charles thought of her more as a kid sister who was fun to be with, until that summer when he suddenly realized he had found the perfect girl.

THE QUEEN MOTHER making her traditional birthday appearance outside Clarence House (above). It was no coincidence that Lady Diana's grandmother, Ruth, Lady Fermoy, was the Queen Mother's lady-in-waiting. The two old ladies were close friends and encouraged a match between their favourite grandchildren. The Queen Mother went out of her way to make meetings possible.

PRINCE PHILIP and the Queen, appropriately dressed in a long black dress, with long sleeves and a black veil, for an audience with His Holiness Pope John Paul II at the Vatican in Rome on 17 October (left). Her position as Head of the Church of England made it a somewhat controversial visit, but the tiara and decorations emphasize her role as head of state, and it was in this capacity that she visited the Holy See. Furthermore the Press were largely diverted by the pursuit of Lady Diana Spencer. Despite the severe expression on the Queen's face – looking more like Queen Victoria than Elizabeth – it was reportedly a friendly meeting.

THE QUEEN MOTHER studying her race-card (above left), while the Queen scrutinizes the runners, at the Epsom Derby. They are both serious racegoers, who make substantial sums of money from their horses. Because she so often watches the race from the same place, the Queen has an unerring eye for knowing, in the event of a photo-finish, the winner. It is the one advantage of having been confined to the royal box, although at Epsom in recent years she has often watched races from the edge of the track.

THE QUEEN leaving Princess Margaret's fiftieth-birthday party (left), held at the Ritz Hotel in November.

WHEN IN North Africa, do as your hosts do. The Queen (above) looks perfectly at ease as she settles down to eat with her fingers at a banquet in her honour, during a state visit to Morocco in October. It was the sixth state visit that she and Prince Philip had made in the space of two weeks, and the first-ever to Morocco, Tunisia and Algeria.

1980

The wedding of Charles and Diana on Wednesday 29 July was the event of the decade. In a break with tradition, Charles had specifically chosen to be married in St Paul's Cathedral. When told that the distance was three times further than the Abbey, and that there might not be enough soldiers to line the route, he simply said, 'Well stand them further apart.'

A public holiday was declared, and in towns and villages all over Britain people partied in the streets, danced, sang, and toasted the royal couple with anything that came to hand. It was hard to believe that just weeks earlier some of these streets had seen bloody and unprecedented scenes of hatred and violence, as a series of riots erupted in some of Britain's crowded and decaying inner cities.

Over 250 million people listened to the ceremony on the radio, and a further 700 million watched it unfold on television, beamed by satellite to seventy nations. Most of the crowned heads of Europe were amongst the 2,650 guests, and over 160 foreign presidents, prime ministers and their wives.

THE QUEEN is sheltered from the heat by a large decorative umbrella (below), during a colourful state visit to Sri Lanka in October. Although she has enjoyed remarkably good health throughout her life, with little more than the occasional recurrence of sinus trouble, extreme changes of heat have at times made life very uncomfortable. From soaring temperatures in Sri Lanka she flew home to the chill of a British winter.

NEWS IN BRIEF

5 Jan – Peter Sutcliffe is charged with the Yorkshire Ripper murders

21 Jan – Iran releases the hostages held in the American Embassy after 444 days of captivity

25 Jan – The 'Gang of Four' issue the Limehouse Declaration, breaking with the Labour Party to form the SDP

30 Mar – President Reagan is wounded in an assassination attempt

4 Apr – Youths clash with police in Brixton, south London

14 Apr – The USA's first space shuttle, *Columbia*, makes its three-day maiden flight

5 May – Bobby Sands, IRA hunger striker, dies

7 May – The Labour Party wins control of the Greater London Council; Ken Livingstone is elected leader the following day

10 May – François Mitterand is elected President of France

13 May – Pope John Paul II is shot and wounded by a Turkish gunman

11 Jun – The Queen opens the Nat West Tower, Europe's tallest building

5 Jul – Rioting erupts in the Toxteth area of Liverpool; urban unrest spreads by the weekend to London, Birmingham, Chester, Hull, Preston, Reading and Wolverhampton

27 Aug – Moira Stuart is appointed the BBC's first black news reader

6 Oct – President Sadat of Egypt is assassinated at a military parade

15 Dec – Martial law is imposed in Poland

THE QUEEN (left) sitting side-saddle on her favourite horse, Burmese, during the Trooping the Colour on 30 June. As she left the gates of Buckingham Palace with a full Guards' escort, a youth in the crowd suddenly opened fire with a gun. Standing just ten feet away, he had a 9mm pistol aimed directly at the Queen. As six shots rang out – which, it transpired, were blanks – Burmese reared, then stumbled, very nearly unseating his royal rider. Thoroughly shaken, but undeterred, the Queen indicated that the ceremony should go ahead, while the youth was promptly arrested.

THE QUEEN escorted by King Olav of Norway, an old family friend of her parents and a distant relative (above). She and Prince Philip were his guests in Oslo during a four-day state visit to the country in early May. Elizabeth was no doubt relieved to have a break from the wedding fever that had gripped Britain ever since the engagement between Charles and Diana had been announced on 23 February. Diana moved out of her flat that day, and went to stay first with the Queen Mother at Clarence House, then at Buckingham Palace.

1981

THE BRIDE and bridegroom (left), return to Buckingham Palace on 29 July after the most expensive wedding recorded in British history. With nearly three million people unemployed and the economy at an all-time low, the Queen had been understandably nervous; but it was a tonic the country needed. As the Archbishop of Canterbury said, it was 'the stuff of which fairy-tales are made.' Church bells burst into life all over the City of London, the crowds cheered, waved and roared their approval, and when the last of the coaches had passed, they flocked like an insurgent army into the Mall for the balcony appearance. Pressed against the railings, they began to chant, 'We want Di, we want Charlie.' Inside the Palace, Patrick Lichfield, was trying to take official wedding photographs in the forty minutes allotted to him. With the help of a whistle to stop the chatter, he made it (below), before Charles and Diana went out on to the balcony. On their fourth appearance they kissed – the first time two members of the royal family had ever kissed on the balcony – and the crowds went wild.

THE PRINCE and Princess of Wales returned from a two-week honeymoon on board *Britannia* to join the rest of the royal family at Balmoral (left) where they posed for photographers on the banks of the River Dee, in the most informal way they have ever done before or since. Charles looked years younger and carefree for almost the first time in his life. Diana simply glowed with contentment. Of married life she said, 'I can highly recommend it. It is a marvellous life and Balmoral is one of the best places in the world.' But even the best places can pall, and as the weeks went by, Diana found that in-laws are in-laws whoever they may be.

1981

THE FAMILY outside church on Christmas morning at Windsor (below). Apart from weddings and funerals, Christmas is one of the rare occasions when so many members of the royal family appear in public together. By this time Diana had announced that she was pregnant.

PRINCESS ANNE with her children, Peter and Zara (left), in the Music Room at Buckingham Palace after the baby's christening. Zara was born on 15 May in the private Lindo Wing at St Mary's Hospital in London, and, like her brother, was a commoner. The name Zara has no significance or royal connotations, and was just a name that Princess Anne and her husband liked. Anne has done a good job in protecting her children from the attention that she herself was plagued by as a child. She has sent them to ordinary schools and made sure they socialize with local children.

*T*he first half of the year was dominated by war against
Argentina in the Falkland Islands, a bloody battle waged
8,000 miles away in the icy South Atlantic. On 2 April, President
General Leopoldo Galtieri of Argentina ordered his army to invade,
and within three hours it had raised the Argentinian flag. Margaret
Thatcher called an emergency debate in the House of Commons on
3 April – the first time the House had convened on a Saturday for
twenty-five years – and two days later the first ships of the task force
set sail. One of the first to go was the aircraft carrier, HMS
Invincible, in which Prince Andrew was serving as a sub-
lieutenant, flying helicopters.

   The battle to reclaim the Falklands cost 250 British lives as ships
went down, Harriers and helicopters plunged into the icy seas, and
soldiers on the ground ran into land-mines and ambushes.

THE QUEEN and Prince
Philip walk down the
gangway of HMS *Invincible*
with Prince Andrew (below),
after welcoming him home
from active service as a
helicopter pilot in the
Falklands War. For weeks,
like every mother with a son
in the South Atlantic, the
Queen feared that any day
Prince Andrew's name would
be amongst the list of dead.

PROUD PARENTS at the christening of Prince William (above) born at 9.03p.m. on 21 June in the Lindo Wing of St Mary's Hospital in London, ten days before Diana's twenty-first birthday. Prince Charles was present at the birth. He became an adept father, and also a dab hand changing his young son's nappy.

THE QUEEN welcoming Pope John Paul II to Buckingham Palace during his six-day visit to Britain in May (right), and clearly looking more relaxed with the pontiff on her home ground than she had during their meeting in the Vatican two years earlier. The Pope's visit was a huge success – his charisma undeniable – and people turned out in their thousands to see him.

THE QUEEN on Burmese with her guest Ronald Reagan (above), about to go for a ride together in Windsor Great Park during the American President's visit to Britain with his wife, Nancy, in June. The Queen has made it her business throughout her reign to develop good relations with most countries – she is Britain's principal Ambassador – but none more so than the United States. And of all the American Presidents that have held office during her reign, Ronald Reagan is probably the one with whom she has had the best rapport, partly because of their shared enthusiasm for horses.

1982

THE QUEEN was in high spirits when she began a tour of the South Pacific. With her customary nerve, she put the frightening events of the summer behind her. On 7 July an intruder called Michael Fagan had found his way into her bedroom at Buckingham Palace, and sat on her bed talking to her with a shard of broken glass in his hand. Soldiers and horses of the Household Cavalry and six musicians from the Royal Greenjackets had been killed by bombs. Now in Tuvulu (above and right), the Queen was greeted as 'Mrs Gwin', and she was carried through the streets in a canoe. In the Solomon Islands (above left) she shook hands with a tribal chief, and in Kiribati (left) was entertained by natives in traditional grass skirts.

N E W S
I N   B R I E F
≈

12 Jan – Mark Thatcher, the Prime Minister's son, goes missing in the Sahara Desert

26 Jan – Unemployment in Britain rises above three million for the first time since the 1930s

19 Feb – John De Lorean's luxury car company is put into receivership

29 Mar – *Chariots of Fire* wins the Oscar for best film

2 Apr – Argentina invades and captures the Falkland Islands

29 May – British troops win the first land battle for the Falkland Islands at Goose Green

9 June – The new 20p coin comes into circulation

14 Jun – Argentina surrenders the Falkland Islands

7 Jul – Michael Fagan breaks into the Queen's bedroom at Buckingham Palace

31 Aug – The PLO abandons its headquarters in Beirut, driven out by Israeli attacks

14 Sep – Princess Grace of Monacco dies in a car crash, aged 52

Sep – Women begin arriving to form a peace camp at Greenham Common, in protest at the proposed siting of US cruise missiles there in 1983

1 Oct – Helmut Kohl is elected Chancellor of West Germany

11 Oct – The *Mary Rose*, a Tudor warship, is raised from the sea bed near Portsmouth

2 Nov – Channel Four opens

10 Nov – President Breshnev of the USSR dies, aged 75; he is succeeded by Yuri Anbdropov

1983

In an atmosphere of mounting speculation about when the Prime Minister would call a General Election, the Queen and Prince Philip flew out of London in the middle of February to join Britannia *in Jamaica. It was the first stop in another eventful tour that took the royal couple through the Panama Canal to Acapulco, and then on to the west coast of America, which the Queen had never visited before. She had never seen such tight security before either. The Queen was accompanied throughout her visit by a permanent bodyguard of 230 secret-service agents, plus local police who were drafted in at every stop. In the event, although there were demonstrations in support of the IRA, they were all peaceful, and it was a most successful trip.*

Back in Britain, the General Election was held on 10 June, and Margaret Thatcher romped home with a huge majority of 144, the first Conservative Prime Minister this century to return to Downing Street for a second consecutive term of office.

THE QUEEN and the Duke of Edinburgh arriving in San Diego in February (below). They were met by unseasonal storms so bad that they were forced to fly instead of sail to San Francisco, where they were guests of the Reagans at an official banquet (below right). 'I knew . . . that we have exported many of our traditions to the United States, but I did not realize before that weather was one of them,' said the Queen.

ON 10 NOVEMBER, the Queen arrived in Kenya (below right), the first time she had been back – apart from a brief touch-down in 1972 – since the visit that was so rudely interrupted by the death of King George VI. Since then, like many countries that had once been part of the British Empire, Kenya had become a republic, achieving independence in 1963 under Jomo Kenyatta, when it joined the Commonwealth.

IN MID-NOVEMBER, the Queen and the Duke of Edinburgh embarked on a major tour of India, during which the Queen attended a Commonwealth Conference, and presented Mother Teresa of Calcutta (above left) with her personal Order of Merit. This was the first time the Queen had been to India since 1961, when she was the guest of Pandit Jawaharlal Nehru, the country's first Prime Minister after independence. Now it was his daughter, Mrs Indira Gandhi (above), who greeted the Queen. She had become India's first woman Prime Minister in 1966, lost power in 1977, and returned in 1980.

17 Jan – The BBC begins transmission of *Breakfast Time*, Britain's first regular breakfast television service

31 Jan – Compulsory wearing of seat belts in the front of cars is introduced

23 Mar – President Reagan announces plans for a revolutionary defence system, dubbed 'Star Wars'

22 Apr – The new £1 coin comes into circulation

1 Jun – Lester Piggott wins a record ninth victory at the Derby

10 Jun – Margaret Thatcher is re-elected Prime Minister

23 Jul – Skirmishes break out on the border between Iran and Iraq

26 Jul – Victoria Gillick loses her High Court battle to prevent GPs prescribing the pill to girls under 16 without their parents' consent

21 Aug – Benigno Aquino, opposition politician in the Philippines, is shot dead at Manilla Airport

6 Sep – The USSR admits responsibility for shooting down the Korean Airlines Boeing 747 flight 007

26 Sep – Australia wins the America's Cup, the first time it has left the USA for 132 years

2 Oct – Neil Kinnock is elected new leader of the Labour Party

5 Oct – Lech Walesa wins the Nobel Prize for Peace

26 Oct – US Marines invade Grenada in a move to stamp out Marxism 'in America's backyard'

17 Dec – An IRA bomb explodes outside Harrods in London

THE QUEEN MOTHER and the Queen with President Kaunda of Zambia and his wife (left) before a state banquet at Buckingham Palace. They arrived in Britain on 22 March.

MEANWHILE, the Prince and Princess of Wales had embarked on a six-week tour of Australia and New Zealand, with nine-month-old Prince William. In Auckland he posed with his parents (below), and stood up on a wobbly pair of legs. He was the first royal baby to have been taken on such a tour, earning Diana great praise from the public.

PRINCESS ANNE
wearing a Save the Children
hat (left) at a celebrity clay-
pigeon shoot in North Wales,
organized by former motor-
racing champion Jackie
Stewart. The previous year
she had undertaken the first
of many punishing and
distressing trips to Africa
and the Middle East as
President of the Save the
Children Fund, visiting sick
and crippled children. The
trip marked a turnaround in
the Press's attitude towards
her. As she herself
remarked, 'I noticed that I'd
undergone a miracle cure'.

ALL THE CHARACTER
and fun caught in the
Queen's face, (above) as she
relaxes with friends and
family in the outdoors.

In March the Queen paid a four-day visit to Jordan, amid unprecedented security. There had been a recent assassination attempt on King Hussein, and there was a risk that the Queen might even be a target herself. It was a year of violence everywhere.

In April British people were shocked when a young unarmed WPC, Yvonne Fletcher, was shot dead outside the Libyan Embassy in St James's Square, and in October a bomb planted by the IRA ripped open the Grand Hotel in Brighton, where senior members of the Government were staying for the Conservative Party Conference: only four people were killed, but many more were seriously injured. And in the same month Mrs Indira Gandhi was assassinated by a member of her bodyguard.

Britain, meanwhile, was once again in the grip of industrial chaos. In March the news that twenty-one pits were to be closed with a loss of 20,000 jobs had brought the miners out on strike. A bitter confrontation against a government determined to break the power of the unions, it lasted almost a year.

IN OCTOBER, the Queen set off for a private trip to Kentucky, where she spent eight days, accompanied by her racing manager Lord Porchester, viewing horses. She also had a day at the races – the Queen Elizabeth II Challenge Cup Stakes horse-race at Keeneland. She was the guest of wealthy Texan, William S. Farish, and his wife, who have a stud farm in Lexington, Kentucky, where one of the Queen's brood mares, High Tower, had recently foaled. The Queen had known her hosts for years: William Farish plays polo with Prince Charles, and they first met in 1973.

THE QUEEN and the Duke of Edinburgh visiting the historic city of Petra (left) during a state visit to Jordan towards the end of March. They spent a morning at the spectacular 2,000-year-old site, wandering freely around the temples, rock tombs and Roman ruins, with their hosts, King Hussein and Queen Noor, to guide them. It was a trip they enjoyed: Hussein is an old friend, and a great Anglophile, but it was nevertheless conducted amid very tight security. There had been a recent bomb attack against their host, who has survived more assassination attempts than he can probably remember, and it was obvious that the Queen could be at risk.

ON A TOUR of Canada in September and October (far left, below). The local Press were unkindly critical of the Queen, saying she no longer drew the crowds, but there seemed to be no shortage of people waving flags, taking snapshots and thrusting flowers into her arms, and no visible lack of enthusiasm for their monarch.

PRESIDENT REAGAN and the Queen (left) exchange a few words at a gathering of kings, queens and heads of state on 6 June for the fortieth anniversary of the D-Day landings in Normandy. President Mitterrand is on the Queen's right.

RECOGNIZED while driving the elderly Vauxhall which she has had for years, the Queen waves (above). She frequently takes the wheel on the short journey between Windsor Castle and the polo at Smith's Lawn in the Park, but a detective always travels in the car with her, too.

THE QUEEN with her guest the Emir of Bahrain, His Highness Shaikh Isa bin Sulman Al Khalifa (right), both looking very cheerful as they travel in an open landau to Windsor Castle at the start of the Emir's three-day state visit to Britain in April.

PRINCE WILLIAM (right) keeps everyone entertained, and especially his royal grandmother, as he clowns about after his brother's christening. Prince Henry, known as Harry, was born on 15 September, and was home with his mother less than twenty-four hours later. Assembled from left to right in the front row are: Ruth, Lady Fermoy; the Queen Mother; the Queen; the Princess of Wales with Harry on her lap; Prince Charles and Diana's mother, Frances Shand-Kydd. In the back row: Lady Sarah Armstrong-Jones; artist Bryan Organ; Gerald Ward; Prince Andrew; Prince Philip; Earl Spencer; Lady Susan Hussey and Carolyn Bartholomew.

*T*he death of President Chernenko of the Soviet Union on 10
March, and the selection of Mikhail Gorbachev as his
successor, heralded the beginning of one of the most exciting
periods in recent world history. But in Britain, riots once again
threatened the safety of the inner cities. The most shocking scenes
took place on the Broadwater Farm estate in north London, where a
policeman fell to the ground and was hacked to death. The violence
was symptomatic of a climate of racial hatred and inner-city
degradation that had become endemic.

*These were maladies that the Prince of Wales had taken on. He
had set up a variety of schemes including a Youth Business Scheme,
and in 1985, a charity to revitalize inner cities.*

A STUDY of the Queen
Mother with four of her
grandchildren taken by
Norman Parkinson for her
eighty-fifth birthday (below).
There is no disguising the
pride and affection that
Charles, Edward, Anne and
Andrew all feel for an old
lady who has been a trusted
friend and confidante to
them all.

NEWS
IN BRIEF

≈

10 Jan – Sir Clive Sinclair unveils
the C5, a battery-assisted, pedal-
powered tricycle

11 Mar – Mikhail Gorbachev
succeeds Konstantin Chernenko,
who died aged 73, as Soviet leader

29 May – Rioting Liverpool fans
leave 41 Italian and Belgian
football supporters dead at the
European Cup Final at Heysel
Stadium, Belgium

7 Jul – Boris Becker wins the
men's singles final at Wimbledon,
the first unseeded player ever to do
so and the youngest-ever champion

13 Jul – Simultaneous Band Aid
concerts in Wembley Stadium,
London, and JFK Stadium,
Philadelphia, raise £40 million

22 Aug – A British Airtours plane
bursts into flame on take-off from
Manchester Airport, the fourth
major air disaster of the summer:
an Air India plane exploded over
the North Sea; a Japanese jumbo
jet crashed into a mountainside;
and an American plane crash-
landed in Dallas during a
thunderstorm

19 Sep – The worst earthquake for
a century leaves thousands dead in
Mexico City

2 Oct – Rock Hudson, Hollywood
heart-throb of the 50s, dies of
AIDS, aged 59

7 Oct – PC Keith Blakelock is
hacked to death by rioters on
the Broadwater Farm estate in
North London

21 Nov – The Geneva summit
meeting between Presidents
Reagan and Gorbachev brings an
agreement to work towards
massive arms reductions

QUEEN ELIZABETH II

1985

THE PRINCE and
Princess of Wales with Bob
Geldof watch the Live Aid
concert at Wembley (left),
which raised millions of
pounds to feed the starving
in Africa. As a lover of pop
music, Diana was in her
element; the Prince was less
comfortable, but his
admiration for Geldof who
organized the event, was
tremendous. The feeling was
mutual. Of all the world's
leaders and politicians that
he met in the course of his
fund-raising, Geldof said,
'I find myself more in
agreement with him than
anybody else.'

THE QUEEN in Portugal
walking on a magnificent
carpet of flowers (left). It was
the first time she and the
Duke of Edinburgh had been
on a state visit to Portugal
since 1957.

THE QUEEN and the
Duke of Edinburgh, dressed
in morning coat and top hat,
leading the traditional
procession of horse-drawn
landaus down the course at
Royal Ascot in June (above).

~ 145 ~

1986

*T*he Queen's sixtieth birthday in April was an intensely happy time for her. Momentarily insulated from the worries of state, she basked in the love of her people and her family. Princess Margaret had organized a special programme at Covent Garden on the evening of the Queen's birthday, at the end of which the audience rose to their feet and joined the cast in saluting the Queen.

In March, much to the Queen's delight, Prince Andrew became engaged to Sarah Ferguson, whose family she had known for years. Sarah's parents were divorced. Her father, Major Ronald Ferguson, had been a polo-playing friend of Prince Philip's, and was now the Prince of Wales's polo manager. Her mother, Susan, was now married to the Argentinian polo professional, Hector Barrantes.

THE QUEEN and the Duke of Edinburgh driving through Windsor on the morning of the Queen's sixtieth birthday on 21 April, on their way to a short service in St George's Chapel (below). Despite the rain, hundreds of people turned out to watch as the team of handsome Windsor greys pulled their carriage, flanked by an escort of the Household Cavalry.

A BIRTHDAY portrait taken by Prince Andrew (left), a remarkable record of a mother's love for her son, and one of the most revealing ever taken of the Queen. Even the Duke of Edinburgh's expression has a softness not often seen in photographs. But since the Duke has been at war with the Press, whom he finds intrusive, for most of his married life, it is hardly surprising. Andrew is the only one of their children who shares the Queen's interest in photography.

ON THE FORECOURT of Buckingham Palace, the Queen is engulfed by a sea of brilliant-yellow daffodils (below) on her birthday. As the Queen appeared on the balcony, children in the Mall burst into song with a specially written birthday composition. The Queen clapped in applause, but was clearly so touched by their display that she decided to come down to talk to the children in person.

NEWS
IN BRIEF

9 Jan – Michael Heseltine, the Defence Secretary, resigns from the Cabinet over a row about Westlad Helicopters; he is followed by Leon Brittan, Trade and Industry Secretary, on 24 Jan

28 Jan – *Challenger*, the US space shuttle, explodes, 72 seconds after take-off

16 Feb – Striking print workers clash with police outside Rupert Murdoch's new printing works at Wapping

25 Feb – Mrs Corazon Aquino is sworn in as new President of the Philippines

2 Mar – The Queen signs the Australia Bill, severing the final constitutional links with Britain

31 Mar – The Greater London Council is abolished

8 Apr – Clint Eastwood is elected mayor of Carmel, California

15 Apr – US F-111s attack Libya, flying from bases in Britain

30 Apr – A nuclear reactor at Chernobyl sets fire

8 Sep – The Japanese car manufacturer, Nissan, opens its new factory in Sunderland

27 Oct – The Stock Exchange experiences 'Big Bang'

29 Nov – Cary Grant, matinee idol, dies, aged 82

30 Dec – Admiral John Poindexter resigns as National Security Adviser and Lt-Col Oliver North is dismissed from the National Security Council following further arms-for-hostages claims in the 'Irangate' scandal

29 Dec – Harold Macmillan, 'Supermac', dies, aged 92

PRINCE EDWARD, in uniform (above). He joined the Marines in September, having graduated from Cambridge in June with a respectable degree in history. In the meantime he carried out his first solo engagement with a tour of Wales for the Duke of Edinburgh's Award Scheme.

THE QUEEN at the Maundy Service (right), held on the Thursday before Good Friday to commemorate the Last Supper. Christ commanded ('mandatum', hence the name Maundy) his disciples to love one another, and for centuries, English sovereigns have given money 'to as many old men and . . . women as the sovereign is years of age'.

THE PRINCESS of Wales with Prince Harry and Prince William (above left) at Aberdeen airport in August, on their way to Balmoral for a family holiday with the Queen. Despite the general formality surrounding the Queen, she is an approachable and indulgent grandmother, and the children clearly feel totally at ease in her company – witness a talkative five-year-old Zara Phillips (left) at the Windsor Horse Show in May. Although there are obvious restrictions on the children, they all enjoy far greater freedom from the disciplines of royal life than their parents ever had as children.

THE QUEEN, Prince Philip, the Queen Mother, Princess Anne and the Prince and Princess of Wales follow the Duchess of Windsor's coffin (above), carried by men of the Welsh Guards, out of St George's Chapel, Windsor, on its way to Frogmore, where she was buried beside her husband on 29 April. She had died on 24 April, aged eighty-nine.

1986

PRINCE ANDREW and Sarah Ferguson were married in Westminster Abbey on 23 July, in a charming ceremony watched by millions. Shortly before the carriages began their procession to the Abbey, a notice went up on the railings outside Buckingham Palace, announcing that the Queen was bestowing on her second son the title of Duke of York. After the ceremony, Sarah would therefore become Duchess. They returned to Buckingham Palace for the customary group photograph (right) taken, surprisingly, by a New York-based photographer, Albert Watson, who had been recommended to the Prince. The entire family then went out on to the balcony (above) where the crowds below, densely packed as far as the eye could see, began chanting, 'We want the kiss, kiss, kiss . . .' So kiss they did (top), to roars of approval from the street.

THE QUEEN and the Duke of Edinburgh visit the Great Wall of China (top) during their historic and fascinating six-day visit in October. The Great Wall, 2,400km long, was originally built by the Ch'in dynasty around 220BC to keep the invading Mongols out. The wall that stands today is a modern version, dating from the Ming dynasty of the fourteenth to seventeenth centuries. The Queen shares a toast (above) with her Communist host in Beijing, and (right) discovers she is a favourite with the children. Also in the party is the Foreign Secretary, Sir Geoffrey Howe.

In March the Queen had been in Australia to sign a proclamation making that country legally independent from Britain. It was rare for her to attend an independence ceremony in person. As one colony after another had broken free during her reign, she had made it a habit to send a representative, such as Prince Philip or one of her children. But Australia was especially close to her heart, and in the wake of Canada's independence, it was the end of an era.

In October, accompanied by the Duke of Edinburgh, the Queen paid a state visit to China, followed by two days that could not have been more contrasting in the capitalist mecca of Hong Kong, the British colony leased from Communist China and due to be ceded back to the mainland in 1997.

THE SPANISH KING, Juan Carlos, and his wife, Queen Sophia, (above) with the Queen and the Duke of Edinburgh, clearly enjoying one another's company at a state banquet at the Spanish Embassy in London, during their first state visit to Britain in April. For years the disputed sovereignty of Gibraltar had kept the families, though related, at an arm's length.

1987

THE PRINCE and Princess of Wales (below), whose marriage had become the subject of intense Press speculation. The strain was taking its toll.

PRINCESS ANNE with actor Kevin Kline (below right), egging their team on in a Grand Knockout Tournament on television. The event, organized by Prince Edward, raised over one million pounds for charity, but attracted severe criticism.

THE QUEEN and the Duke with Prince William, Prince Harry, and Peter and Zara Phillips (opposite).

*T*his was a troubled year, starting with Prince Edward's decision in January to leave the Marines. Not long afterwards he was given a job by Andrew Lloyd Webber in his Really Useful Theatre Company: it was an unusual departure for the royal family, and the Duke was predictably furious. He would have liked all his sons to be rough, tough action men, and had hoped that Edward would be less of a disappointment than Charles in that respect; but the Queen and the remainder of the family were supportive, and respected his courage in speaking out.

For some time there had been rumours that Princess Anne's marriage was in trouble, but now it seemed that Charles and Diana were also unhappy. They spent so much time apart during the summer that by the end of the year speculation about a divorce was so rife that there were even questions asked in the House of Commons about the potential constitutional implications.

In June Margaret Thatcher called a General Election, and was re-elected for a third successive term, making her the longest-lasting Prime Minister of the century. Most people prospered under her regime, but the poor and underprivileged suffered great deprivation and were treated with little compassion.

N E W S

IN BRIEF

≈

12 Jan – Prince Edward resigns his commission from the Royal Marines

21 Jan – Terry Waite, envoy of the Archbishop of Canterbury, is reported missing in Beirut

2 Feb – Special Branch detectives raid BBC offices in Glasgow and seize tapes for a programme about the Zircon spy satellite

22 Feb – Andy Warhol, American Pop artist, dies, aged 58

6 Mar – The *Herald of Free Enterprise* car ferry capsizes, killing up to 200 people

5 Apr – Mary Whitehouse claims that the low moral values of the soap opera, *Eastenders*, put viewers at peril

12 Jun – Margaret Thatcher wins a record, third General Election

20 Aug – Michael Ryan shoots dead 14 villagers and then himself in Hungerford

4 Sep – A West German man is given four years in a Soviet labour camp for landing his plane in Red Square

16 Oct – Hurricane-force winds overnight devastate the south of England

19 Oct – Shares crash on the London Stock Exchange, on what becomes known as Black Monday

8 Nov – An IRA bomb kills 11 at a Remembrance Day service in Enniskillen

18 Nov – Fire sweeps through King's Cross tube station, killing 30

8 Dec – Presidents Reagan and Gorbachev sign the first-ever treaty that reduces the size of their nuclear arsenals

1988

The year got off to a tragic start with the death of Major Hugh Lindsay – swept to his death by an avalanche at Klosters in Switzerland – which shocked the entire royal household. Hugh Lindsay was well known to them all. For the past three years he had been one of the Queen's equerries, and the family had all been at his wedding the year before, when he married Sarah Brennan, who was now six months pregnant, and had stayed behind while her husband went skiing with the Prince and Princess of Wales.

It marred what was otherwise a joyful year, with the birth of a daughter, Princess Beatrice, to the Yorks; and Prince Charles's fortieth birthday in November, which he celebrated with 1,500 young people who had been helped by the Prince's Trust.

THERE IS NO disguising the warmth and affection as Prince Charles kisses his mother's hand (right) when she presents him with a prize at the end of a polo match at Windsor. Charles adores his mother, and they are alike in many ways, not least in their sense of humour, and, of course, their love of horses. Often criticized for playing too much polo – three or four times a week during the season – many of the matches he plays are for charity. In the last fifteen years the Prince reckons he has raised no less than £3.8 million for various causes.

PRINCE CHARLES gives his grandmother a steadying hand as she negotiates the steps of St George's Chapel, Windsor, in her flowing robes, after the annual Order of the Garter Ceremony in June (opposite, left).

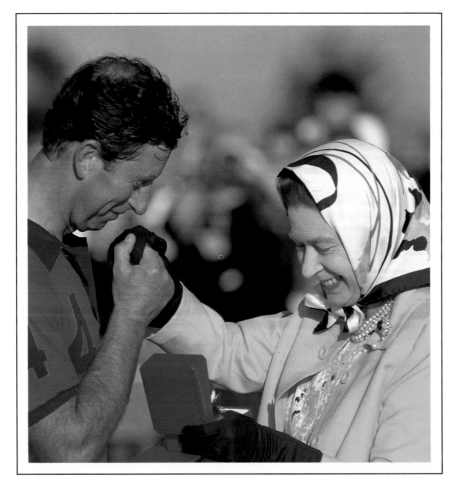

NEWS
IN BRIEF
~

5 Feb – Red Nose Day in Britain marks Comic Relief's campaign to relieve famine in Africa

9 Feb – MPs vote to experiment with the televising of parliament

7 Mar – SAS soldiers gun down three members of the IRA in Gibraltar

16 Mar – At the funeral of the IRA members killed in Gibraltar, a Unionist gunman opens fire, killing a further three

19 Mar – Two British soldiers in West Belfast die at the hands of a lynch mob

3 Jul – A US guided missile shoots down an Iranian airbus over the Gulf, killing 286

6 Jul – A massive explosion rips apart the Piper Alpha oil rig

8 Agu – Two ceasefires are announced: one between South Africa and Angola, the other between Iran and Iraq

28 Oct – Prince Charles's BBC *Omnibus* film attacking modern architecture is broadcast

8 Nov – George Bush wins the US Presidential election

30 Nov – Benazir Bhutto is elected Prime Minister of Pakistan

10 Dec – More than 100,000 people are feared killed by the earthquake in Armenia

16 Dec – Edwina Curry resigns as junior health minister following her claim that most British eggs are infected with salmonella

22 Dec – Pan Am flight 103 is blown apart by a bomb over the Scottish town of Lockerbie, killing at least 270 people

TROOPING the Colour for the last time on her favourite mount, Burmese (top). As the horse was due to retire, the Queen retired from the saddle herself.

A SOBER PARTY of the Prince and Princess of Wales and the Duchess of York (above) return from Klosters with the body of their friend, Hugh Lindsay.

PROUD PARENTS: the Duke and Duchess of York with Princess Beatrice (far left) after her christening at St James's Palace in December. The baby was born on 8 August, and six weeks later the Duchess left for a tour of Australia, which she extended to spend a holiday with Prince Andrew. Beatrice was left at home in the care of a nanny; and the Duchess, who had been a popular addition to the royal family, came under fire.

REMEMBRANCE Sunday, and a solemn Queen (left), a red poppy in her lapel, stands at the Cenotaph in Whitehall for the salute of guns, followed by a minute of silence. Formerly called Armistice Day, it was renamed Remembrance Sunday, when the service became a fixture on the second Sunday in November.

THE QUEEN looks decidedly anxious as she and Princess Anne, both dressed in the same dazzling yellow, watch the Derby from the Royal Box at Epsom in June (left). Minutes later, however, her arms were out-stretched in triumph, as, yet again, she picked a winner: Kahyasi, owned by the Aga Khan, romped home to win at 11-1 odds. Sitting alongside her is the Queen Mother; also in the box were Prince and Princess Michael of Kent, and the Duchess of Gloucester.

ON 14 NOVEMBER, the Prince of Wales celebrated his fortieth birthday in a converted tram shed in Birmingham (left), where he sportingly took to the floor for a dance. The party was thrown by the Prince's Trust, which Charles set up while in the Navy to help young people such as the unemployed trainees who had restored the disused old depot and turned it into a transport museum. Wearing a '40' badge on his lapel, Charles cut a three-tiered cake, then took to the floor.

In April President Gorbachev arrived in London on a three-day state visit, and had lunch with the Queen and the Duke of Edinburgh at Windsor Castle. His reforming policies of perestroika and glasnost; his final withdrawal from Afghanistan at the beginning of the year; his resolution to reduce the Soviet armed forces by 500,000 and cut its armaments; and his promise to tackle environmental pollution and third-world debt had won him strong approval and respect in the West. These actions had also been inspirational for the peoples of Eastern Europe.

The result was a year of dramatic political change, as the Communist leaderships in Hungary, Czechoslovakia, Poland, Yugoslavia, Romania and East Germany began to collapse one after another, in the face of growing demand from their citizens for democracy. Only in China did the government remain firm. What began in May as a peaceful sit-in by students demanding political reform ended in carnage as tanks moved in to Tiananmen Square, and massacred an estimated 2,500 people.

THE QUEEN reading the menu at a state banquet during her visit to Kuala Lumpur in October (below). She was in Malaysia for the Commonwealth Conference. Opening the Conference, the Queen compared its composite countries with her own family. 'Like all the best families, we have our share of eccentricities, of impetuous and wayward youngsters and of family disagreements.'

SENSITIVELY dressed in a long coat and a hat (below), the Queen has points of interest explained to her during a visit to a mosque while she and the Duke of Edinburgh were in Malaysia.

N E W S
IN BRIEF

~

23 Jan – More than 1000 people are killed by an earthquake in Armenia

2 Feb – The last Soviet troops leave Afghanistan

5 Feb – Sky TV, Britain's first satellite network, is launched

14 Feb – The Ayatollah Khomeini issues a *fatwa* against Salman Rushdie, author

24 Feb – Prince Philip is among world leaders attending Emperor Hirohito's funeral in Japan

15 Apr – Ninety-four football supporters are crushed to death at the Hillsborough FA Cup semi-final

4 Jun – Tanks pour in to Tiananmen Square, massacring protestors

6 Jun – The Ayatollah Khomeini, leader of Iran, dies

11 Jul – Laurence Olivier, the first actor to be created a peer, dies, aged 82

14 Jul – Spectacular celebrations in Paris mark the 200th anniversary of the French Revolution

31 Aug – Buckingham Palace announces the separation of Princess Anne and Captain Mark Phillips

11 Sep – Hungary opens its border to allow East Germans to flee West

19 Oct – The Court of Appeal sets free the Guildford Four

26 Oct – Nigel Lawson resigns as Chancellor of the Exchequer

10 Nov – The Berlin Wall is opened

24 Nov – The Communist government of Czechoslovakia resigns

25 Dec – Nicolae Ceausescu, Romanian dictator, is executed

A SPECTACULAR line-up of Guards parade outside Windsor Castle (above), where the Soviet President, Mikhail Gorbachev, and his wife, Raisa, were lunch guests of the Queen and Prince Philip during their visit to Britain in April. In the course of their meeting the Queen accepted an invitation to visit the Soviet Union at a future date.

1989

A WARM WELCOME for the Queen (above) on her sixty-third birthday from the pupils, teachers and parents of Dunraven Primary School at Treherbert, in Mid Glamorgan. The Queen and the Duke of Edinburgh visited the school during a trip to Wales in April.

THE QUEEN on her way to the Palace of Westminster (right) for the annual State Opening of Parliament. Westminster is the oldest royal palace, where Edward the Confessor, who reigned from 1042–66, spent his last years in order to be close to the Abbey he had founded. The original building was burnt down, but although it now houses Parliament, its replacement is still in theory the monarch's principal residence.

ADDING WEIGHT to the campaign for lead-free petrol (left), the Queen met children sporting campaign sweat-shirts in the Royal Mews at Buckingham Palace. The Queen announced that all royal cars which were modern enough to be converted to take the more environmentally friendly fuel would be adapted. As well as polluting the atmosphere, lead emissions from cars have been linked with damages to the IQs of children, but, despite the evidence, for years Britain lagged behind her European counterparts in persuading the public to change. However in March, the Chancellor of the Exchequer provided the first real incentive to the public by making lead-free cheaper than leaded petrol in the Budget, and since then there has been a marked reduction in lead emissions.

THE QUEEN takes shelter under canvas during a visit to a regiment of Gurkhas based at Church Crookham (above). This elite infantry unit of the British army, named after the Nepalese ruling dynasty, recruits from the hill tribes of Nepal, and has fought in campaigns all over the world for more than one hundred years, from battles on the North West Frontier of India in the nineteenth century, through the Western Front in World War I, and the Burma and Italian campaigns of World War II, to the Falklands War in 1982. Traditionally led by British officers, they still carry Kukris, the characteristic fighting knives with curved blades.

The year saw a series of landmark birthdays. Princess Anne and Princess Margaret reached forty and sixty respectively; and the Queen Mother was ninety on 4 August.

In the same month, Saddam Hussein, Iraq's military dictator, invaded the small oil-rich kingdom of Kuwait and deposed the ruling family. And after the boom of Margaret Thatcher's reign, Britain had hit a recession. Michael Heseltine, her former Defence Minister made a direct challenge to Mrs Thatcher's leadership, and in the ensuing ballots in November, the Queen found herself with a new Prime Minister in John Major.

THE SUN SHINES *for the Queen Mother as, surrounded by her family, she waves to the crowds outside Clarence House on the morning of her ninetieth birthday on 4 August (below). To the left of Princess Anne are her son, Peter, and Viscount Linley.*

DELIGHTED BY THE mysteries of a helium balloon (left), the Queen Mother moves forward into the crowd gathered outside Clarence House to talk to the children who have proffered it as a birthday gift.

THE QUEEN with her mother, attending a special Birthday Gala at the London Palladium (above). The Queen Mother's birthday gave rise to long and lavish public and family celebrations as her loyal and adoring fans paid tribute after tribute to a grand and splendid figure.

1990

THE QUEEN experiences the extraordinary conditions around Iceland's thermal springs (above), during her first-ever visit to the country at the end of June. Despite the cold climate – all but one per cent of the island is covered in ice – the Icelanders make use of the thermal springs for hot-house cultivation.

THE PRINCESS ROYAL sightseeing during her trip to the Soviet Union at the end of May (right), where she opened the 'Britain in Kiev' exhibition.

THE QUEEN inspecting the 5th Airborne Brigade on Salisbury Plain in May, to mark the Brigade's fiftieth anniversary (left). Three months later, British troops began moving into the Gulf as part of a multi-national force which would, if necessary, remove Saddam Hussein from Kuwait. Conditions were difficult in the desert, and it was a long and tense wait for the troops, as Prince Charles discovered during a visit in December. He is pictured (below) in a tank belonging to the 7th Staff Regiment in Saudi Arabia.

1990

THE DUKE and Duchess of York leaving the Portland Hospital (opposite) after the birth of their second daughter, Princess Eugenie, born on 23 March.

THE QUEEN amongst friends during a visit to Eton College for the school's 550-year celebrations in May (left). She is accompanied by the Provost, Sir Martin Charteris (wearing the surplice), who for many years was her Private Secretary. The headmaster, Dr Eric Anderson, (to the right of Charteris) taught Prince Charles at Gordonstoun, and in time, he may well teach Prince William, too.

A HOST OF ROYAL faces turn to the sky, on the balcony of Buckingham Palace in September (below). They are watching a fly-past to commemorate the fiftieth anniversary of the Battle of Britain. No fewer than 1,733 German aeroplanes were destroyed in the most decisive battle of World War II. Britain lost 915 aircraft. Watching with the Queen, the Duke of Edinburgh, Princess Margaret, the Duchess of York, the Princess of Wales, Prince Harry and the Duchess of Kent, are members of the Belgian and Dutch royal families.

On 17 January allied forces from countries including Britain, America and Saudi Arabia went to war in the desert to force Sadam Hussein's army out of Kuwait. The conflict was short-lived, and allied losses were kept mercifully low.

In April the Queen celebrated her sixty-fifth birthday. Showing no sign of retiring, as some people had expected, she took off to the United States for a state visit, where she was fêted by President Bush in Washington. With visits to Namibia and Zambia in October, and a full domestic diary for the remainder of the year, the Queen was scarcely even slowing down. In June the Duke of Edinburgh was seventy, and appeared genuinely surprised and pleased by the celebrations in his honour, the tributes, and the affection the public so clearly felt for him.

POLISH PRESIDENT
Lech Walesa is clearly interesting company as he and the Queen drive in a state landau through Windsor Great Park in April (above). Dozens of Poles were there to greet the President, the former electrician from the Gdansk shipyards and leader of Solidarity. For ten years he had relentlessly fought for his country's freedom from the totalitarian regime in Poland, and been imprisoned in the course of it. He and his wife were in Britain for four days on a state visit.

1991
1952~1992~2
1952~1992~

IN MAY the Queen and the Duke of Edinburgh embarked on a hugely successful visit to the United States, starting in Washington, where the Queen was greeted rather over-enthusiastically (above) during a stop at the Drake Palace Housing project. President George Bush adhered to procotol and kept his distance (top right) when receiving the Churchill Award; as did General Norman Schwarzkopf (above right), who commanded the allied forces in the Gulf, when he was awarded a KBE.

THE QUEEN and the Duke of Edinburgh chatting during the Gulf Parade in the City of London in June (left). Jubilation at victory in the Gulf was considerably tempered by the continuing problem of the Kurds, who had begun a mass migration to the frontiers in the north of Iraq, fleeing for their lives from the murderous forces of Saddam Hussein. On 10 June, the Duke had celebrated his seventieth birthday, and was honoured with a special birthday parade in Hyde Park, a gun salute and a fly-past.

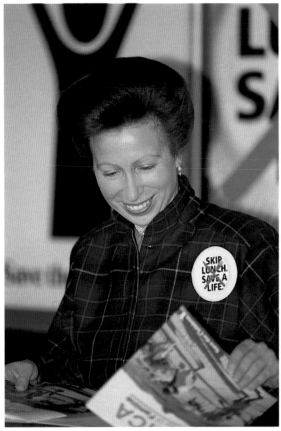

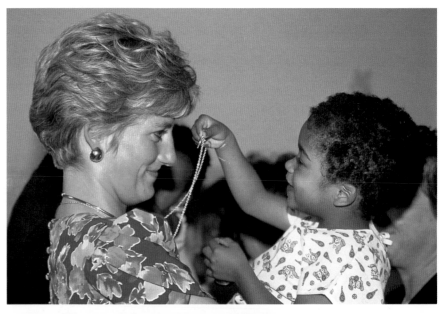

THE PRINCESS Royal (above) at the launch of a major campaign to raise money to relieve famine in Africa. In a most direct and sincere appeal, broadcast on television, she asked people to 'Skip Lunch and Save a Life', by giving what they would spend on lunch to help feed the millions starving to death in the war-torn regions of Sudan and Eritrea, which were suffering from one of the worst famines this century.

THE QUEEN MOTHER during a visit to Guy's Hospital in February (right), just six months away from her ninety-first birthday, and going strong. She not only continues to look magnificent, but she is still performing public duties at a rate of three or four in some weeks, a good thirty years after the official retirement age for women.

DURING a visit to a hostel for abandoned children in Sao Paulo, Brazil, the Princess of Wales (above) holds a young child who is HIV positive. It was not the first time she had publicly made physical contact with HIV-positive or AIDS patients, and she has done much to still public fear of the disease by practising what she preaches.

DERBY DAY in June with a difference (right). The occupants of the Royal Box are all engrossed in the racing as usual, but capturing the excitement for posterity is a BBC camera-man, filming over the Queen's left shoulder, for a major documentary on Elizabeth II to commemorate the remarkable, fortieth anniversary of her accession.

Acknowledgments

The publisher thanks the following photographers and organizations for their kind permission to reproduce the photographs in this book:

1 Hulton Deutsch Collection; **2** Snowden/Camera Press; **4–5** Richard Open/Camera Press; **6** Karsh of Ottawa/Camera Press; **7** Tim Graham; **10** Tim Graham; **13** Photographers International; **14** left Hulton Deutsch Collection/Keystone; **14** right Topham Picture Library; **15** Popperfoto; **16** above Hulton Deutsch Collection/Studio Lisa; **16–17** below Hulton Deutsch Collection; **17** left Topham Picture Library; **17** right Popperfoto; **18** Popperfoto; **19** Cecil Beaton/Camera Press; **20** above Hulton Deutsch Collection; **20** below Topham Picture Library; **21** Popperfoto; **22** Joe Waldorf/Popperfoto; **23** left Hulton Deutsch Collection/Keystone; **23** right Topham Picture Library; **24** Popperfoto; **25** left Rex Features; **25** right Popperfoto; **26** Popperfoto; **27** left Topham Picture Library; **27** above and below right Popperfoto; **28** Hulton Deutsch Collection; **29** left Annigoni/Camera Press; **29** right Topham Picture Library; **30** Popperfoto; **31** above Topham Picture Library; **31** below Popperfoto; **32** Popperfoto; **33** above D. Moore/Camera Press; **33** below Popperfoto; **34** Popperfoto; **35** left Hulton Deutsch Collection/Fox; **35** right Hulton Deutsch Collection; **36** Camera Press; **37** above left Popperfoto; **37** above right Topham Picture Library; **37** below Popperfoto; **38** above Express Newspapers PLC; **38** below Topham Picture Library; **39** left Hulton Deutsch Collection; **39** right Jack Esten/Camera Press; **40** Studio Lisa/Camera Press; **41** above left Camera Press; **41** above right Topham Picture Library; **41** below Camera Press; **42** left Cecil Beaton/Camera Press; **42** right Popperfoto; **43** left Cecil Beaton/Camera Press; **43** right Camera Press; **44** Hulton Deutsch Collection; **45–6** Popperfoto; **47** above left John Bulmer/Camera Press; **47** above right Hulton Deutsch Collection; **47** below Topham Picture Library; **48** Daily Herald/Syndication International; **48–49** Popperfoto; **50** left Popperfoto; **50** right Hulton Deutsch Collection; **51** Hulton Deutsch Collection; **52** Popperfoto; **53** left Popperfoto; **53** right Rex Features; **53** below Hulton Deutsch Collection; **54** above Popperfoto; **54** below Hulton Deutsch Collection; **55** above Hulton Deutsch Collection; **55** below Popperfoto; **56** above Hulton Deutsch Collection; **56** below Cecil Beaton/Camera Press; **57** Rex Features; **58** Hulton Deutsch Collection; **59** Topham Picture Library; **60** Camera Press; **61** left Camera Press; **61** right Topham Picture Library; **62** Hulton Deutsch Collection; **63** above left Camera Press; **63** above right Hulton Deutsch Collection; **63** below Express Newspapers PLC; **64** above Rex Features; **64** below left Popperfoto; **64** below right John Bulmer/Camera Press; **65** Popperfoto; **66** Hulton Deutsch Collection; **67** above left Anthony Buckley/Camera Press; **67** above right Express Newspapers PLC; **67** below Popperfoto; **68** above Topham Picture Library; **68** below Hulton Deutsch Collection; **69** Anwar Hussein; **70** left Hulton Deutsch Collection; **70** right Camera Press; **71** Camera Press; **72** above Popperfoto; **72** below Hulton Deutsch Collection/Fox; **73** above Hulton Deutsch Collection/Fox; **73** below left Popperfoto; **73** below right S. & G. Press Agency; **74** Keith McMillan/Camera Press; **75** Hulton Deutsch Collection; **76** Popperfoto; **77** above Popperfoto; **77** below Hulton Deutsch Collection; **78** Press Association; **79** above Anwar Hussein; **79** below Rex Features; **80** Popperfoto; **81** Camera Press; **82** above Rex Features; **82** below Popperfoto; **83** above Camera Press; **83** below Rex Features; **84–5** Popperfoto; **86** Patrick Lichfield/Camera Press; **87** above Hulton Deutsch Collection/Bippa; **87** below Topham Picture Library/Press Association; **88** left Goksir Sipahiglu/Rex Features; **88** right Popperfoto; **89** Tim Graham; **89** above right Colin Davey/Camera Press; **89** below right Hulton Deutsch Collection; **90** Patrick Lichfield/Camera Press; **92** Tim Graham; **93** above Camera Press; **93** below Associated Press; **94** above left Norman Parkinson/Camera Press; **94** above right Serge Lemoine/Sygma; **94** below Tim Graham; **95** Camera Press; **96** Popperfoto; **97** Hulton Deutsch Collection; **98** above Press Association; **98** below Serge Lemoine/Sygma; **99** above left Anwar Hussein; **99** above right Press Association; **99** below Serge Lemoine/Sygma; **100** Hulton Deutsch Collection; **101** Peter Kain/Camera Press; **102** Hulton Deutsch Collection; **103** above Hulton Deutsch Collection; **103** below Popperfoto; **104** Anwar Hussein; **105** above left Tim Graham; **105** above right Photographers International; **105** below Hulton Deutsch Collection; **106** above Rex Features/Sipa; **106** below Photographers International; **107** above Anwar Hussein; **107** below Photographers International; **108** Photographers International; **109** above Hulton Deutsch Collection; **109** below S. & G. Press Agency; **110** Camera Press; **111** above left Camera Press; **111** above right Express Newspapers PLC; **111** below Rex Features; **112** Anwar Hussein; **113** left Camera Press; **113** right Malak/Camera Press; **114** Tim Graham; **115** Anwar Hussein; **116** Photographers International; **117** above left Tim Graham; **117** above right Anwar Hussein; **117** below Photographers International; **118** Anwar Hussein; **119** above Tim Graham; **119** below left Photographers International; **119** below right Camera Press; **120** Tim Graham; **121** above left Hulton Deutsch Collection; **121** above right Peter Abbey/Camera Press; **121** below Topham Picture Library; **122** Norman Parkinson/Camera Press; **123** left Rex Features; **123** right Tim Graham; **124** Tim Graham; **125** above left & below Photographers International; **125** above right Anwar Hussein; **126** Photographers International; **127** left Tim Graham; **127** right Photographers International; **128** above Photographers International; **128** below Patrick Lichfield/Camera Press; **129** Hulton Deutsch Collection; **130** Patrick Lichfield/Camera Press; **131** above Photographers International; **131** below Anwar Hussein; **132** Anwar Hussein; **133** above right Photographers International; **133** above left Topham Picture Library; **133** below Photographers International; **134** above Anwar Hussein; **134** below Anwar Hussein; **135** Anwar Hussein; **136** left Tim Graham; **136** right Photographers International; **137** Anwar Hussein; **138** Photographers International; **139** left Photographers International; **139** right Jim Bennett/Camera Press; **140** left Photographers International; **141** above Tim Graham; **141** below right Photographers International; **142** above Photographers International; **142** below Tim Graham; **142–143** Snowden/Camera Press; **144** Norman Parkinson/Camera Press; **145** above Rex Features; **145** below left Anwar Hussein; **145** below right Tim Graham; **146** Photographers International; **147** above HRH Prince Andrew/Camera Press; **147** below Rex Features; **148** left Rex Features; **148** right Photographers International; **149** above left Photographers International; **149** above right Tim Graham; **149** below Anwar Hussein; **150** above Photographers International; **150** Tim Graham; **150–151** Albert Watson/Camera Press; **152** above left Mauro Carraro/Rex Features; **152** below left & right Anwar Hussein; **153** Photographers International; **154** left Rex Features; **154** right Photographers International; **155** Karsh of Ottawa/Camera Press; **156** Tim Graham; **157** left Anwar Hussein; **157** above right Anwar Hussein; **157** below left Rex Features; **158** Tim Graham; **159** above left & below Rex Features; **159** above right Tim Graham; **160–1** Tim Graham; **162** above Anwar Hussein; **162** below Tim Graham; **163** left Tim Graham; **163** above right Photographers International; **164** Brooker/Jorgensen/Rex Features; **165** left Brooker/Jorgensen/Rex Features; **165** right Camera Press; **166** left John Shelley/Camera Press; **166** right Rex Features; **167** above Tim Graham; **167** below D. Hudson/Sygma; **168** Jorgensen/Rex Features; **169** above Photographers International; **169** below D. Bubble/Camera Press; **170** Photographers International; **171** above left Photographers International; **171** below Anwar Hussein; **172** Rex Features; **172** above right Tim Graham; **172** below Camera Press; **173** Photographers International.

Every effort has been made to trace copyright holders and we apologise in advance for any unintentional omission and would be pleased to insert the appropriate acknowledgment in any subsequent edition of this publication.

AUTHOR'S ACKNOWLEDGMENTS

I would very much like to thank all those people in the Press Office at Buckingham Palace who have answered an endless stream of questions and queries, identified people and places from photographs, and generally been enormously helpful, as always.

Celia Deering has done an amazing job in finding such interesting and revealing pictures – and so many of them. I would also like to say a special thank you to photographer Jayne Fincher, who has been a great help, and to Simon Willis at Conran Octopus, who has also been tremendously helpful, and a pleasure to work with.

Of the many books I have consulted on the subject, the following were particularly helpful, and my thanks to their authors and publishers:
MAJESTY by Robert Lacey (Hutchinson, 1977)
ELIZABETH AND PHILIP by Charles Higham and Roy Moseley (Sidgwick and Jackson, 1991)
TRIBUTE TO HER MAJESTY by Don Coolican (Windward/Scott Publishing, 1986)
THE QUEEN OBSERVED introduced by Trevor Grove (Pavilion Books, 1986)
MOUNTBATTEN by Philip Ziegler (Collins, 1985)
ANNE, THE WORKING PRINCESS by Paul James (Pan Books, 1988)
PEARS' CYCLOPAEDIA edited by Chris Cook (Pelham Books, 1990)
TRAVELS WITH A PRINCESS by Jayne Fincher (Weidenfeld and Nicolson, 1990)